About the Author

Donna Collins is a Transpersonal Psychotherapist. She has a private practice in Hertfordshire and London. She also has an undergraduate degree in Psychology from the Open University. She specialises in working with those experiencing spiritual emergence as well as a broad range of clinical presentations.

Donna has been inspired to write this book following her own spiritual awakening in 2011, which occurred spontaneously following the passing of her father, Paul. Her experience was life changing and prompted her to follow her own soul purpose, changing her career and retraining as a Transpersonal Psychotherapist, as well as facilitating groups focused on energy healing and soul alignment.

Donna brings together her spiritual wisdom, knowledge of psychology and experience of psychotherapy in her first book.

Faith in Everyday Life

*Living Consciously From
The Heart*

Donna Collins

Copyright © Donna Collins, 2021

Donna Collins has asserted her right to be identified as the author of this Work in accordance with the Copyright, Designs and Patents Act 1998

All rights reserved.

No part of this publication may be reproduced, stored in a retrieval system, or transmitted, in any form or by any means, without the prior permission of the author, nor be otherwise circulated in any form of binding or cover other than that in which it is published and without a similar condition including this condition being imposed on the subsequent purchaser.

Published in the United Kingdom

ISBN 979-8-53225-419-0

Dedication

This book is dedicated to my father, Paul, who passed away in 2011. His gifts were life, loyalty to family, and on passing, spiritual awareness.

Also to my mum and sister, who have supported me with their own Faith and Trust in our shared spiritual journey since then. I thank you from the deepest place in my heart. Without your support and belief in all that we experienced at that time and since, this book may not have been written.

To my wife Nadia, who was dedicated in her enthusiasm and support as I wrote this book, and has inspired me to continue to write through all the emotions that were experienced in every chapter!

I would also like to thank my dear friends at Darley Dale Spiritualist Church who unconditionally gave their love, healing and support, as well as their kindness and friendship during the early stages of my spiritual journey, and continue to do so.

Lastly, to my close friends and family who have supported and encouraged me throughout this journey.

Contents

Foreword	1
Introduction	6
Faith	27
Ego Consciousness	52
Emotions	76
Love	90
Creativity	99
Surrender Through the Heart	114
Grace & Harmony	136
Trust & Truth	155
Beauty & Magnificence	177
Gratitude	196
Being Light in the Everyday	205
Being Faith	225
Bibliography	229

Breathing techniques & practices

Listening to your Heart breathing technique	32
Light breathing technique	49
Going Back to Ourselves practice	57
Freedom breathing technique	63
Befriending the ego practice	71
Simple breathing technique	72
Re-framing terminology practice	83
Breathing with Emotions technique	85
Ask yourself the *Love* question	97
Imagination practice	100
Love Flowing Through the Heart practice	103
Listening to the Birds practice	149
Sensing the Energy Field practice 1	218
Sensing the Energy Field practice 2	219
Energetic body self-healing practice	220
Transforming Emotions daily practice	222

Visualisations

Tree	36
Beach	46
Grounding into the Body	73
River	87
Experiencing Love within	95
Wonderment	108
Deer Encounter	110
Meadow	128
Soul Purpose	129
Light of Grace Through the Leaves	137
Feathers	142
Breathing in the Multiverse	152
Trusting & Floating Downstream	168
White Horse	175
Smiling at Beauty	178
Experiencing the Flowing Stream of Compassion	184
Inner Masculine & Feminine	190
Mountain Top Gratitude	197
Listening to the Stillness	210

Foreword

A spiritual message

In the summer of 2015, I was visiting my mum at her home for my birthday. The weather was warm and the sky was a brilliant pure blue. Mum was occupied in the house temporarily and I sat waiting in the conservatory. The sun was shining down on me through the glass doors. I looked out at the garden I knew so well, a place that my parents had spent so much time in together before my dad had passed. They had worked, as my mum had shared, 'as a team' together for many years to create a garden they were truly passionate about.

Their love for each other and for nature inspired them to nurture the garden and this love was reflected in the perfectly manicured lawn and immaculately kept borders with a plethora of plant species including roses which had been gifts from family and to each other over the years.

Donna Collins

My parents' favourite birds, the robin and the blackbird, were not in my present view but memories of the three of us sitting together in this room, drinking tea and watching all the birds, formed images in my mind.

As I sat, I became more aware that the pain of bereavement was starting to subside, and that I was able to access wonderful memories instead. The sun was becoming warmer on my skin and I felt nurtured by it; I could sense the healing of my pain through my body and I felt the beauty of my surroundings, and love and gratitude in my heart.

In that moment, I had a profound, energetic, heart-opening experience. Intense emotion swept over me like a wave. It felt like pure love pouring through my heart. This love felt so much bigger and expansive than my heart was able to contain. I started to feel vibration through my body, a pulsing that I struggled to control. It was immense and I struggled to catch my breath. The purity of the love felt overwhelming and tears filled my eyes and rolled down my cheeks.

A knowing filled my consciousness. I became aware that my purpose was to teach. I stood up in an attempt to let the energy flow more easily through my body. I was still struggling to manage the intensity of the force that now seemed centred around my heart.

I opened the conservatory door and stepped outside. I walked onto the grass and took off my shoes as a means of grounding myself, a technique I had learnt over the last four years since my awakening had begun.

I took a deep breath down into my stomach and breathed out. The sensation of the grass seemed to soak up some of the energy pulsing through my body and I felt calmer. I walked slowly, looking at the apple tree that my parents had planted over 30 years before.

As I began to feel more at ease with the amount of vibration and emotion, I asked aloud, 'What should I teach?'

I was aware of the words, 'The way.'

'The way' being the way of the spiritual path.

That is the reason this book was written, for what I hope will be the furthering of personal and spiritual awareness for us all.

Along with this realisation came a further knowing. A wisdom about who we all really are, as spiritual beings in a physical body. This book is for us all to take some time to remember.

Donna Collins

The following words flowed through me at that time:

*Beyond light and colour is an intense light
which is creation.
We are all light.
Light is Wisdom, Love and everything in existence.*

Emotion is the way we connect with the light. Love is the highest vibration we can achieve in the physical. We feel it so strongly with experiences we call 'spiritual'.

The soul is the light space experienced by man as Love.

Trees and plants are significant. They show us the importance of light. They have light sensitive cells in the same way that we do.

The way light manifests in the body is what we call the 'soul purpose'.

We sometimes see this as different colours, which some call the 'aura' or as the colours of a rainbow or reflected in prisms.

This is the frequency given by God, which cannot be altered. The physical body can deny it, but it is impossible as this is the whole life purpose.

Love is God's guidance and our true nature.

During those moments, I managed to write down what I was hearing to allow me to remember and share them in this book.

After I had written the words, the energy started to subside. Over the coming days when I reflected on my experience I realised this was a significant furthering of my spiritual awakening that had first begun in 2011.

This time however, it appeared more specific. I had become more aware of my purpose. The way had been made clear to me.

This experience brought a deep, continuing Wisdom within me. I was now clear of my path. A passionate creativity flowed through my being. I was going to share this Wisdom in order to help others experience their own soul, their own Light through the heart.

Introduction

Why?

For a number of years after my spiritual awakening, friends and acquaintances often suggested I should write a book to share how my awakening had changed my life, both inwardly and externally.

I considered the possibility of this, and my conclusion and response was always *maybe*. At that time, I also felt that perhaps I wasn't ready. There was still more to experience which might need to be included in a book, so this sense of unfinished work meant I refrained from writing.

Eventually, by continuing to walk my own spiritual path and through many years of hard work in my own personal therapy, I realised that there is no such thing as unfinished. There was not going to be a specific event or a full stop somewhere in my life that would mean I was ready to write! The only final moment in this physical existence would be when I died, and that would clearly be too late!

I reflected on the past and remembered that my awakening had brought a lot of fear. The catalyst had been my father's passing, which in itself had been destabilising as it is for many. The devastating realisation that my reality since birth had changed forever as my dad was no longer in the physical was intertwined with a new, instantaneous awareness of the fabric of reality itself.

I had opened, in a moment, to a new way of functioning.

My life before was very different. I worked in finance. I had followed in my father's footsteps at it were; he was an accountant and I had somewhat haphazardly found my way into finance too, by default almost, by losing my job due to a company going into liquidation and a friend telling me all those years ago that 'one of the big insurance companies was hiring.'

And so, I found my way into finance. The most enjoyable aspect of it was meeting people and as I progressed, working from home and interacting with clients were the most enjoyable part of my work.

I had been away on a training course in Cheltenham on the day of my dad's death. I had a phone call from my sister in which there were no other words than 'Dad's died.' I left immediately, against all the advice being given to me by the training staff at the time. I drove directly to my parents' house to find the police outside.

The scene inside will never leave me; my mum and my sister were sat on chairs crying. My dad's body was lying on the floor where he had collapsed an hour before. I found myself telling my sister it was going to be alright as I walked in but of course it wasn't. My dad's body was kept in the same place he was in, after paramedics were no longer able to revive him.

My mum had requested my dad's body not be moved until I arrived in order for me to say goodbye. Saying goodbye to a dead body is the most incredibly disturbing act. The pain and love and fear that wells up inside all at once is overwhelming.

I found myself feeling very afraid as I had never seen a dead body before. What was striking was that it was very clear my dad was no longer present. His body was clearly there but any conscious presence was not. Everything about him had changed. This was not the same as seeing someone asleep; this was seeing someone who had gone.

I touched my dad's hand and felt shocked at how cold it was. I told him I loved him. There were no other words to say.

My mum then also held my dad's hand and to my surprise, she said, 'We will be watching for you.'

That night, after my dad's body was taken to the undertakers, my sister and I slept in the living room whilst my mum slept upstairs. Neither of us felt we could go to bed even though there were spare beds to sleep in.

I experienced immense fear. What was most striking was that I did not want to close my eyes, at all. I had a strong sense that I would see more with my eyes closed than with my eyes open.

I didn't know what this meant at the time; I was too overwhelmed with grief that was really starting to move through my body as the realisation that my dad had died sank in.

I did not know it then, but I have since learnt that grief is a doorway to spirit. In some North American Indian cultures those who are grieving are considered most awakened and stand on the threshold of the spirit world.

All of our ego defences, our self-limiting protection, can be blown away in a moment and if that happens, everything changes, if we allow it. And this is what happened to me.

Donna Collins

The following day the three of us were trying to get through the morning, all intermittently crying as well as trying to focus on funeral arrangements and notifying family members.

I sat opposite my mum in the afternoon and she talked about her pain at not being in the house when my dad had collapsed as she was visiting a neighbour. Mum was wondering out loud how it must have been for my dad.

In that moment, I found myself opening my mouth and telling my mum exactly how my dad had felt. With no conscious thought, I simply spoke the words until we both stopped speaking, shocked.

Something happened in that moment, a realisation that somehow I knew something that I couldn't possibly have known as I wasn't in the house at the time.

Neither of us were able to process what had been said. We simply focused on getting through the pain and grief of the coming moments. Later, I went upstairs, intending to have a shower.

Something was happening to me, a growing sense of a presence that was somehow greater than me. In that moment I paused. I didn't get in the shower; I sat in the chair in my parents' room instead. I knew I had to sit and listen. I had no idea what I was listening to exactly but I did just that.

I realised I wasn't listening with my physical ears. There had been a shift within me, a remembering. I was listening with my heart. It was like a magnet being drawn to another magnet, something it resonated with so well – like an irresistible pull that feels very familiar, a sense of home.

This pull in my heart took me to my parents' wardrobe. I felt like a detective looking for clues to a greater story that I didn't know yet, a subtle feeling of not being able to just walk away. I called my mum and asked her if there was anything in the wardrobe that was important and she said no. I tried to turn away but the draw in my heart was too strong. I opened the door and reached along the rail to a tie hanger at the end. Hanging on it was my dad's gold watch. He had hidden it there as my parents were meant to be going on holiday in two days' time and he wanted to keep it safe.

I had no knowledge of this and yet somehow I was being drawn to know. In that moment I began to wonder if this *draw* was also a means of communication.

What followed was weeks and months of communication; the draw in my heart, which I started to recognise was energy, also became visions as well as words that I heard always in my right ear. I also felt energy as emotion, which I was able to transmute into conscious thought. The communication was constant.

This was very intense and overwhelming as I was also still experiencing grief. I started to see energy, in the form of white mist moving through the room, as well as Light and colour around objects, such as trees and plants and other people. I found this very scary at first and I slept with the light on for the next two years.

I sought out help from a spiritualist church in Derbyshire who normalised my experience for me. A wonderful medium there, who is also now a friend, said to me the first time I walked through the doors, 'Your dad has brought you here so that we can help you.'

I learnt that my dad's energy was the *draw* in my heart and I was also shocked to hear that I was a medium. I hadn't considered that other energy besides my dad's could also communicate in the same way.

Learning to function with all my new awareness took years of practice. I had many sleepless nights, shouting out in fear as energy moved in and out of the room. I regularly saw the energy or spirit of those who had passed, mostly in the form of people in my mind but also sometimes externally.

I started taking part in spiritualist church services and eventually took the services myself. Sharing my visions was a relief as it gave me the confirmation that what I was seeing was not my imagination and that I was not going crazy. When I shared these experiences and what spirit was telling me, it always brought profound healing for other people as it meant so much to them.

I had also experienced in the early days of awakening, many hours of channelling words of inspiration and Wisdom as well as seeing spiritual beings and I continued to receive communication and guidance from my dad.

I also had moments of seeing the world with heightened senses. The colour and light was intensified, like being in an animated movie or as if I'd in some way been plugged in and power boosted!

The overwhelming feelings gradually subsided over time. I continued to work as a medium and at the same time, I started retraining as a psychotherapist. I also began facilitating groups to help others learn to open to energy.

During this time I also experienced moments when I lost my sense of physicality. I became pure awareness, which is both a blissful and terrifying experience.

I started to realise that I was also energy. I was spirit in a physical body and all my focus until this time had been on energies outside of myself. The beautiful Light that I had seen in visions, through spiritual beings, angels and beautiful gardens attuned in perfect harmony was also within me as I realised I was not separate in any way.

Through the growing, calming Wisdom of what I had been through, I gradually started grounding back into my body with a new strength. I was now strong enough and able enough to start writing about this experience in order to help others.

Now there was no sense of waiting until I had the final piece of information or experience to write about as I knew the reality of the universe as endless and full of infinite possibilities for human beings to experience. And yet I was still hesitating.

I realised that I was delaying writing due to one simple, yet hugely challenging, factor and that was my own fear. My fears that I had experienced when I had first awakened were being triggered in me. Fear of judgement and being labelled and fear of being different had now also become fear of how my book would be received and fear of not being a good enough writer.

I recognised this fear both in myself and also over the years in my work as a psychotherapist, I had observed that every client I worked with was being held back by fear. As well as the work I was doing with clients, I also noticed that fear was scattered throughout society through every means of mass communication, including some religious doctrine, mainstream television, radio, the internet and social media.

It occurred to me that the vast majority of people, if not all, are using fear-based reasoning in the form of excuses and distractions. I considered one particular client, whom I had worked with for a number of months. Her challenge was that it was very difficult for her to hold boundaries in her very high-paced and stressful job.

As we continued to work together it become apparent that this client had deep, unconscious feelings of inadequacy and fear of not being good enough, which stemmed from her childhood. In order to compensate for this and at the same time distract herself from these feelings she was unconsciously driven to have a high-powered job that kept her from her family and caused huge anxiety.

Her psyche not only kept reaffirming her false beliefs about herself but also kept her re-experiencing her fears and prevented her from achieving her aim of a work/life balance. In other words, her unconscious was actively creating the very thing she was in therapy to try to prevent.

Donna Collins

As I contemplated this and my own fear of writing this book, I also wondered what else we are all distracting ourselves from.

I recalled again several years earlier when I had a significant spiritual experience, which contained an intense shift in awareness.

I was visiting my family at Christmas. I had gone upstairs to my room in the evening to get something and as I walked into the bedroom I was aware that it was dark outside and I had a thought that I needed to put the light on so that I could see what I was looking for.

That last thought was not followed by any action. Instead it was as if someone had pressed pause. I recall stopping where I was, not intentionally but spontaneously, and suddenly it was as if I had completely disappeared, I was not aware of my own body at all.

My body had gone, the room had gone. I was no longer seeing through my physical eyes – no sound, no smell, no physical senses and no thought – and yet I was still aware, not of anything physical. I was aware of a great void, like an abyss; there was nothing material in it and yet it was immense in terms of what seemed like endless darkness, a knowing, a greatness, an expansiveness, and what stays with me so vividly now as a place of beauty in my heart, was an incredible sense of stillness, peace, a place of rest and a place that felt like home.

I had spontaneously shifted awareness outside of my own ego consciousness and became pure knowingness. I am using the term 'ego consciousness' in this instance to describe the human perception of our identity and existence as a separate entity.

There was also no sense of time at all. Therefore I'm uncertain how long I was there. There followed another moment when it seemed as though my conscious mind was reinstated and my sense of my physicality returned. I was suddenly back within ego consciousness, aware of my senses and the room I was in and that something incredible had just happened.

As instantly as the experience of someone pressing pause on my conscious mind happened, it was as if someone had again pressed play.

It was only when I shifted back into the consciousness of my ego and my body that I began to experience intense fear. My ego felt a threat to its separateness, and my body reacted with an adrenalin-induced fight, flight or freeze response.

Ultimately, my ego was doing its job of ensuring I survived as a separate being, keeping me away from experiencing my true nature as a spiritual being, connected with all things in the universe.

It is only now with experience that I have the wisdom to know how important and significant our ego consciousness is. Without it, I would not be able to share my experience with you.

Outside of ego consciousness, we do not have the capacity to speak or write or have any awareness of ourselves physically to interact. We simply are awareness itself and so my experience brought with it huge gratitude at being able to share the importance of ego consciousness, particularly as many spiritual teachers suggest otherwise.

I experienced the important concept that ultimately spirituality in the everyday is being able to integrate these two hugely different experiences, that of spirit and matter, our spiritual selves and our physical selves. In our physical life, here in the human body, we need both to function on this earth.

Initially at least, in order for the ego to carry out its job of survival, it has to forego the ultimate experience that most on the spiritual path are searching for: the experience of our own greatness, our own Light, our own limitlessness.

I realised following that experience that the very thing that spiritual seekers are searching for is around us and within us all the time.

As I considered the reasons for not writing my book, I was reminded again that this sense of separateness and smallness filters down into every decision we make, and the emotion that the ego utilises to ensure this happens is fear.

This fear is felt in many forms – as loneliness, insecurity, a sense of being different, isolation, and often arrives with its friend anxiety.

So, I was not writing my book due to one significant factor: I was afraid of my own greatness and I am not the only one….

I reflected on my work as a psychic, a medium and energy healer, an instant ability I also became aware of at the beginning of my spiritual awakening. I knew I was not learning something new; I was remembering the full extent of what it is to be human.

The sensation of needing to sit and listen when my dad passed, I knew now, with experience, was listening to a greater part of me – a greater, infinite source of energy and Wisdom.

My experience also helped me to realise that this is something that is innate within all human beings. We are something much greater than, bigger than we realise.

Most people simply do not understand how to get there because their own ego consciousness is busy creating distracting thoughts and fear in order to sustain their own sense of separateness.

These two factors were facing me now: firstly as a fear of writing and secondly, uncertainty (another form of fear) of how to get there, where to start…

Ironically, in order to write, I had to overcome the very thing I wanted to write about.

How?

I reflected on my spiritual experiences and my work with energy. In order to do this work, I had needed to learn to get out of the way of myself. By that I mean that I had to recognise when my fears were running the show. I would know this when self-doubt and a lack of confidence happened.

Ego consciousness does not just step back when asked. It's far too clever and complex than that. Through my training as a therapist, I had learnt that the ego only responds to kindness, compassion and understanding of why it exists.

This was something I had to implement now in order to write.

I also needed something else, something profound, something I knew because I had glimpsed the Wisdom and Beauty of it over the last nine years of intense spiritual experience.

I needed to trust in something greater than me. I needed to trust that there was something flowing through me that was calling me to write in the first place, and in doing so I would have Faith in myself and my book and in my own everyday life.

Once I knew this, it became clear that the content of my book was going to differ to that which I had imagined.

Initially, I had considered, as suggested by others, writing a book that would share my experiences of the last nine years of spiritual awakening.

I began to recognise that reading about my personal experiences may help others to normalise their own spiritual experiences; however, it would not help people transform their own lives.

I reflected on other experiences and again my work as a medium, in particular the services I had been conducting on a regular basis in spiritualist churches.

Donna Collins

I remembered a philosophy I shared during a service in 2019 at a wonderful spiritualist church in Derbyshire, where I first went when I began my spiritual awakening.

During this particular philosophy, the words flowed through me, which I described at the time as 'instructions for happiness in everyday life'.

Recalling this philosophy sparked a sense of excitement within me. The joy experienced through the body when the soul starts to respond. I realised that what was missing in people's lives and what would really help people transform their lives was something beautifully simple – something that would help people gradually change their everyday experience if they started to implement it.

In short, an instruction manual – just the same as something that would be used for any machine or technical equipment but for ourselves, as human beings, trying to integrate spirituality into our everyday lives.

I had read many books on spiritual awakening and spirituality, and although I had found them useful, I had never found a book that gave practical advice on how to integrate spirituality into everyday life itself. In fact, there appeared to be no obvious structured societal help for me during my awakening. This caused extreme difficulties and a huge sense of loneliness for me and many others I encountered who were also experiencing spiritual awakening.

The view of many at the beginning of a spiritual journey, including myself, is that spirituality is something loving, beautiful and serene. Often experienced as something distinctly different and apart from life in the physical – literally heaven, separate to earth, which creates a sense that life is dull and dense and in some ways pointless.

I saw many people in spiritual development groups I belonged to who had had spiritual awakenings as I had and many, like myself, struggled with the confusing question of what to do with this new awareness. We were all wondering how we could use this new wisdom to help ourselves in life now.

When I shared these challenges in spiritualist churches, many people nodded their heads and looked relieved as they were experiencing the same thing.

What was missing was the very thing that I had needed, a book to help people integrate spirituality into everyday life, not reaching 'up there' for something seemingly unreachable but something within that can be reached by everyone. Something that the modern world could relate to. Put simply, a way of bringing us closer to an experience of heaven on earth.

Donna Collins

This philosophy forms the basis of this book, which also includes how to put into practice many of the things I needed to implement in order to start writing.

It is my vision that those who are drawn to this book will be at a stage in their lives where they are being called to change and transformation, and are being drawn to a sense that there is something greater than themselves.

I hope that this book is able to provide support and can introduce a way of living and breathing spirituality in each day.

Each chapter describes the experience of certain aspects of Faith, including inspirational words that have flowed from my own heart, and specific practices, such as visualisations and techniques for interacting and relating to yourself, as well as encouragement to practise and implement these consciously in the everyday.

The visualisations can be done via simply remembering the text; alternatively, it is also possible to record them yourself and play them back so that you can relax into the experience. They are also available to download at **www.donnacollins.net**.

If you are not drawn to visualisations, I would instead suggest reading them and allow yourself to creatively draw what you are being guided to imagine as an alternative.

There is no right or wrong in this kind of practice. The more you can allow yourself to simply experience what is, the more a true reflection of your inner world they will become. So I would recommend you simply enjoy practising!

Before starting any of the practices, I would recommend that you have privacy and that you are safe to close your eyes and focus your attention inward, so sitting down and being still is important!

It can be helpful to keep a journal so that you can refer back to your experiences during the visualisations and your drawings. Keeping notes about your feelings and insights in your journal as you go along can really help you to see how you have transformed throughout this journey, remembering that Faith in everyday life is a life-long journey for you to enjoy.

At the end of each chapter there are specific practices which will help you open to experiencing the qualities of the Light within. I describe these qualities as Light frequencies, which you can imagine as different colours. As you experience more of these qualities, perhaps you could include some of your own unique qualities in addition to those mentioned in this book! It is possible to energetically begin to create your own inner spectrum of Light, or we could call this your own Rainbow.

When held and experienced in your heart, these frequencies of Light will enable you to learn how to nurture your soul and open to experiencing Faith in each day.

Symbolically, we can imagine that we can become the fullness of a tree with an inner strength that thrives and blossoms when immersed fully by its roots into the earth and by its branches and leaves as it grows up into the Light.

A note about God

I refer to the word 'God' many times throughout this book. This word is used as a means to capture the innate pure consciousness that is within all things in the multiverse, including that which we cannot see. It is used as a word that captures something that is within us all, and can be viewed as the true Self, as well as something that is also greater than ourselves, that we connect to, that some experience as things such as nature or the multiverse. The word 'God' is not used with any religious connotations.

I wish all readers of this book unconditional Love on your journey to your own Truth and Love within and Light on your path to Faith in everyday life.

Chapter One

Faith

To go boldly with Trust in your Heart

To understand how we integrate Faith in daily life, I feel it is necessary to first consider what Faith actually means.

Faith is often misunderstood as religion and I have experienced conversations in social circles, with friends and acquaintances, in which people seemed to switch off from the subject when the word 'Faith' was mentioned despite the fact that it is a concept that can potentially bring so much joy.

So first, assuming you have continued reading, what do I mean by Faith? To me, Faith is not religion. It has no assumed right or wrong beliefs. It has no story line or origin in a person who has lived before. It has no doctrine on how to live your life in order to avoid some foreboding place.

It may be helpful in this moment to consider what Faith currently means to you?

In my experience, Faith is trust in the Self. It is trust in an inner knowing, the felt sense that there is something bigger flowing through us that is beyond our physical limitations, an inner strength and feeling at the very core of us that enables us to carry on believing that there is more to life than the mundane of everyday tasks. It is the part of us that still believes in magic, the part of us that gets whisked away in the flow of things when we are truly present, that literally gets us into 'the spirit of things'.

It is a place of pure joy and unconditional Love, and at the same time a place that brings peace, calmness and fortitude.

This joy comes from an awareness of what and who we truly are, first and foremost. It is the knowing and Wisdom within, brought about through experience of our own Light.

The word 'Light' is a word I have often heard during transpersonal psychotherapy sessions when clients are able to access something within themselves that they had previously forgotten. They often describe, through facilitated visualisation, something they sense in their body, often in their heart space, which they can only describe as Light.

In these moments, the client experiences something profound. It is like a wave of Truth washing over and through them with immense Beauty. In these moments, I know that the client has accessed something within themselves that is much greater than they ever imagined they were before and ever believed they could be, and this is the moment they begin to transform their lives. It is a magical moment when both myself and the client experience the feeling of Beauty and unconditional Love.

One particular experience of this was when I was facilitating a client access her inner essence via visualising that she was a tree. I asked her to focus her attention on what was inside the tree. She immediately responded that she saw gold Light within the tree and I asked her to notice where in her body this would be to which she placed a hand on her heart.

I asked her to describe the Light by focusing on going into it. She described it as very warm and powerful. She then said, it's much bigger than me but it is me too. She then shared without prompting, it's eternal.

The client was so focused on the tree she did not realise what she was describing until the visualisation came to an end and I was able to help her see that she was describing her own inner Light. The Truth of who she was had been experienced by her in the session.

This helped her to recognise that she was so much more, so much stronger, than she had previously believed she was and it reassured her that she was not alone.

Through these experiences, and my own, I have come to understand that the word 'Light' has many meanings.

If you and I were both standing looking into this beautiful Light, trusting it, allowing it to wash over and through us, we would experience other facets of this beautiful essence: one being Love, the other being a sense that within this Light is the ultimate, undeniable Truth of all that is. It feels warm, creative, expanding and powerful, and at the same time is also serene, peaceful and calm, and beautifully reassuring, nurturing and accepting.

In many people, other qualities are also felt in these moments that are unique to them; however, in my experience, the same main qualities are felt by different individuals time and again.

The idea of Light for some is misunderstood as physical light, such as we see from the sun, or lights in our houses and on our streets. This light is not the Light I am referring to now. I am talking about the Light that is termed by many spiritual traditions as Divine Light, the Light of all Creation and that same creative Light is within us… always. Why?

Because it is the very thing that we are. We have simply forgotten through life experience.

Awareness of this Light within enables us to live our lives differently, using the Light as inner guidance. It's very subtle, so it takes practice to learn to listen to it in a different way to using our physical ears. The gateway to this Light is through our heart space. I refer to the heart in this way as it is not accessed through the physical heart – it is something beautifully subtle and energetic that comes through what some traditions refer to as chakras, specifically the heart chakra or in Sanskrit, the 'Anahata' or heart centre. It also requires trust that it is ever present in all we do and is the make-up of all that we are. It is this trust that is intricately entwined into Faith itself.

Listening to your Heart breathing technique

As you are sitting, reading this book, pause and close your eyes, taking your attention within. Notice where within is for you. Focus on your breath, breathing right down into your stomach.

Notice where any tension is being held in your body and focus on breathing in and out of these places, letting that tension go.

Now taking your attention down to your heart. You may notice initially your physical heart. Now take your attention to a space that feels like it is behind the heart.

Focus on breathing in and out of this space. Notice what this feels like.

Stay in this space for a few moments, simply enjoying the sensation of being there. You may initially feel an expansion in your chest; this is normal, simply breathe into the expanding space.

Then gently bring your awareness back into the room, back to this book, back to your body and when you are ready, take a couple of deeper breaths and open your eyes.

This practice can bring a sense of expansion as you start to experience your energetic self or your *Light*. This is perfectly normal. I would encourage you to practice this frequently as you work through this book.

One of the main factors that restricts people from experiencing their own Light is life experience. Over a lifetime many impressions are placed on us, based on both implicit and explicit messages given to us by others we meet, as well as cultural and societal messages which form the foundations of who we believe we are.

This can be viewed as what the psychologist Donald Winnicott called the 'false self' and is part of how our psyche or ego consciousness constructs beliefs about ourselves, meaning we start to function in specific ways in order to protect ourselves and survive in the world.

I have seen many examples of this in a therapeutic setting. I have often observed clients who initially appear very introverted and shy. They often find it difficult to express themselves and often ask me if what they are saying makes sense.

Over the course of the therapy, it is often brought to light that the client has experienced a parent or care giver being very harsh and critical in their response to them when they were young.

What I see in the initial stages of therapy is an adult who has learnt to adapt themselves, becoming quieter and low in self-esteem and confidence. They have become a false version of themselves, a quieter, inward-focused version that was created in order to avoid harsh, critical responses. Being quiet meant being left alone.

This is an example of how, throughout life, we begin to forget who we really are, as a being of Light. We begin to experience emotions such as loneliness and a sense of isolation and thoughts of something missing. That something is our Light and re-experiencing this Light is the beginning of the path towards wholeness and Faith in everyday life…

We can begin to glimpse our Light by learning to relinquish the layers of untrue self-beliefs that keep us from this inner awareness. This is done by discovering what the ego, our psyche, has learnt to believe about itself that is untrue, which is discussed in the following chapter.

We can also use practices such as meditation and guided visualisation, which can give us a means of looking into our inner being, beyond the ego mind.

The following is a visualisation that you can practise in order to start to experience your inner spiritual essence. I would encourage practising this visualisation as you continue through this book to experience any changes in awareness.

I would suggest starting by sitting either in a chair or on a cushion on the floor. I don't usually recommend lying down for visualisations as generally people fall asleep! This is absolutely fine when listening to a guided visualisation as it is still possible to experience the energy of the visualisation being transferred or channelled through the person guiding. However, for visualisations done alone, try sitting.

I would also recommend creating a beautiful space that is yours in which to sit. Some guidance I once read that was shared in a beautiful book called *The Heart of Meditation* by Swami Durgananda, suggested honouring the space in which you meditate, which again can be anything from on a chair to a cushion.

This is a practice I learnt to implement years ago. Eventually, I realised with a smile on my face that this is the practice of starting to honour yourself and every experience you have. I found myself feeling Love and affection towards my meditation cushion every time I looked at it and eventually realised it had become an object that mirrored myself! A cushion that showed me my own frequency of Beauty and Love. I am still in awe of this experience, so again I would encourage you to consciously choose a cushion or chair or simply a space that you always meditate in.

Donna Collins

Visualisation: Tree

To begin, sit in a comfortable chair with your feet flat on the floor. Notice how your toes feel today. Notice the sensation of the floor supporting your feet and the chair supporting your body. Breathe slowly down into your stomach.

Imagine you are walking in a beautiful meadow, surrounded by nature, hearing the sound of the birds and feeling the gentle breeze against your skin. Notice what it is like to be there, using all your senses.

Ahead of you, you see a row of trees and notice yourself being drawn to one particular tree. You walk up to the tree, noticing the bark and how the branches and leaves reach up to the light.

Now take your attention to what is inside the tree. Notice the qualities of the tree. What colour is it inside? What does it feel like?

Now take your attention deeper into the colour, into the feeling. What else do you sense is there?

Take a few moments to really get to know this space.

When you're ready, take a couple of deeper breaths, bringing your attention back to the room that you're in. Breathe in and bring your attention back to your body, and your beautiful meditation space. Open your eyes, coming back into the place that you started in.

When you have finished the visualisation, I would encourage you to write down what you experienced and draw the tree if you feel you would like to. Then take some time to reflect on the fact that everything you experienced about and within the tree is you. This can be difficult to digest initially so take your time and notice if you have any resistance to it. This will be your ego fearing your Light.

Faith in another

With the new awareness of yourself as Light, and perhaps an emerging understanding of and compassion towards yourself for the reasons why you forgot your own Light, it is then possible to start to recognise the same thing in others.

The distorted view of the Self impacts on how we treat others and how they treat us. If someone says something to hurt you or acts in a way that is painful to you, they are really showing you the pain in themselves. They are behaving in a way that is out of alignment with their true nature, their Light, and ultimately away from Love.

I will say more about this in Chapter 3 on Emotions to give a better understanding. However, what I mean by this is that our life experience, especially our childhood experience, affects the way we see the world and how we relate to others in our adult lives, especially in close relationships.

Donna Collins

The hurt and pain we experience as children in early relationships often shows itself in how we perceive and respond to those close to us in later life. So our adult behaviour is often a reflection of a deeper pain that is unhealed within. This pain is a layer over our Light as it has impacted on our memory of our true Self.

Once we start to see that close relationships are mirrors into everything that covers over our own Light, we can work with this in relationships in order to become more conscious of ourselves and our truth, and in intimate relationships, our partner can do the same. This is the essence of a conscious relationship.

The first step to this is for both partners to take responsibility for what is happening within them and not to blame the other for their responses. We can also understand and empathise with the motivations for the behaviour of another as we know that it is their own life experience that creates their chosen conscious or unconscious response.

An example of this is a female client I worked with who struggled with her husband's responses to domestic tasks in the home and her interactions with their son who was still a toddler. This was especially around meal times. Her husband would make suggestions of how to cook or how to stop their son throwing food.

My client experienced an intense emotional reaction to this. She shared with me that she found her husband's comments really upsetting. Through exploring my client's early childhood and home life growing up with her parents, it came to light that her father had been hugely critical and would sometimes use both verbal and physical means to reprimand her if she did not do something right at home.

My client internalised this criticism and developed a false core belief about herself that she was not good enough.

When her husband said something about her behaviour in the present, my client was re-experiencing the pain of her childhood experience. In effect, her unconscious mind was perceiving her husband as her father and his comments were crushing for her as they also reaffirmed her false belief in herself.

Once this was brought to consciousness my client was able to see that her husband's intentions were to help her. He was not her father and she was not being punished, and she was in fact more than good enough. She was a very capable person with many qualities.

When she was able to share this with her husband he was also able to understand and give my client space to do things in the home without commenting and Trust her to do what she felt was the right thing. They were also able to work together with their child. Both of them were then able to speak openly about what they felt was the best way of parenting without a sense of blame or criticism.

Having this level of Faith in another can help us to respond to their difficult or challenging behaviour, not in terms of condoning it, but in terms of an understanding, which ultimately alleviates the level of pain we then attach to it. This is what happened for my client.

Sometimes this is intensely difficult and we will often experience the behaviour of another as hugely painful. We can return to our own Light when we learn to forgive.

Forgiveness

I have experienced many people in psychotherapy sessions struggling to forgive someone who has hurt them. This is totally understandable as the pain experienced in many interactions with people close to us can be overwhelming.

Forgiveness does not mean making a certain behaviour of another OK. It is not a means of saying to another, 'It's alright to do that again…'

Forgiveness is the act of letting go of pain in order for us to move back into awareness and live in alignment with our own Light and ultimately Faith in each day.

The understanding that Forgiveness is for *you* first and foremost, helps many people start to feel more comfortable in forgiving and lets them choose to start to free themselves from the difficult emotions and pain that has been holding them back.

Forgiveness happens in three stages:

1. Understanding

Understanding does not mean making things OK. It means considering the other person's position, considering where are they at in terms of living consciously. Are they still in an unconscious, painful place where they simply are not aware of the behaviour they are displaying? Or have they forgotten themselves and their Light so much that they would intentionally behave in a certain way in order to feel better?

It is at this point that many people in therapy start resisting forgiveness and share that they really don't care where the other person is at. They initially therefore resist having understanding for others.

When I hear this, I know it is an attempt to hold on to the pain of the experience. The reason this happens is that although it is painful, the psyche holds on to this pain in order to reaffirm the false beliefs about who we are as a person.

When I explain this concept to clients, many respond by saying 'Why would I do this to myself?!'

The answer is because the psyche fears the concept of change more than the pain of believing something that isn't true. It has identified with these beliefs and thinks this is who we are.

It may seem unbelievable; however, the psyche finds the belief in something that is painful less scary than the fear of who we may be if we are not what we mistakenly believe we are. In my experience with clients, people are always something greater than they imagine, and the psyche is always scared that it may become nothing when we begin the work.

In the previous example, if my client had not been open with her husband, she would have continued to feel crushed by his comments and this would have reaffirmed her core belief of *not being good enough*.

Understanding ourselves and other people means that we reduce the potential for being continuously caught up in blaming and we do not hold on to the pain and unconscious core beliefs about ourselves.

So if you are experiencing resistance to considering things from another person's perspective right now, I encourage you to make the conscious choice to start to let go, to free yourself of the pain that you hold on to in order to move towards the experience of inner freedom, peace and the Love and joy that you truly are.

2. Compassion

Understanding another person's circumstances and possible reasons for behaviour is the first stage because generally, in order for change to happen, it requires a willingness and a level of conscious thought first. For real transformation to happen, however, this understanding has to be felt in the heart, as empathy and ultimately as compassion.

The extent of our empathy and compassion for others often arises through the wisdom of our own experience. We empathise at a deeper level, with an inner emotional resonance, when we have experienced a similar thing ourselves.

For example, experiencing bereavement is what many would describe as a catastrophic event. The reason it is described like this is in an attempt to acknowledge the hugely traumatic loss in people's lives both in the present and in the future, as well as the destabilising effects that bring huge fear for many people. This leaves people wondering *how will I manage?*

Donna Collins

When we hear of a person struggling because they have suffered a bereavement, we are able to both understand intellectually what this might be like, and if we have experienced a bereavement ourselves we are able to remember what it felt like for us, and therefore resonate and *feel* for the other on a deeper emotional level too.

If we have not had the same experience, we gain this emotional resonance through the capacity to imagine as much as possible what it might be like for the other person, by feeling and therefore resonating with their experience.

By practising being open to the willingness to pause and try to understand someone else's circumstances, we open the door for us to also feel on a deeper level what this might be like for them.

These acts take us a step closer to forgiveness.

This is a hugely important step, because forgiveness is also something we need to learn to give to ourselves. If you practise these steps when others do something that hurts you, then when you make a mistake, when you act in a way that in hindsight you would not have chosen, it is possible to also have understanding and compassion for yourself.

We can learn therefore to forgive ourselves, and forgive others, no matter how difficult it may seem.

These steps are the key to returning to the frequency of Light.

3. Acceptance

When we accept, we stop blaming others; we stop feeling angry and hurt. We stop trying to work out *why?* Acceptance is the penultimate stage prior to forgiveness as when this happens, space is created energetically in the body for forgiveness to enter.

Experiencing forgiveness

Once we have experienced the first three stages, forgiveness is known through a felt sense in the body – a relief, a letting go of a heaviness, a subtle shift which is often experienced as starting to look towards the future, a gentle smile that comes with a thought of what was.

We know we are through something when we gain the capacity to reflect, which tells us we have let go of the painful feelings. Sometimes it may be necessary to revisit these stages in order to completely let go, and sometimes it will be necessary to have some help, such as therapy, particularly if there was some experience of trauma.

We may also utilise alternative means of letting go and the following is a beautiful visualisation practice to enable you to gradually – or instantly – do this.

Donna Collins

Visualisation: Beach

Sit comfortably on a chair with both feet flat on the floor, or on a cushion on the floor, with your back supported.

Taking your attention within, breathe right down into your stomach, gently breathing in and out, noticing the rhythm of your own breath.

Imagine walking along a beach. Imagine breathing in the fresh air, the sound of the breeze and the waves flowing in and out, the sun shining down on your skin.

Now imagine pausing for a moment, standing still and turning round. You notice that a long way behind you on the beach are the people in your life that have caused you pain.

Really allow yourself to experience the feelings attached to the experience of these people.

Then imagine yourself taking a deep breath and turning and facing forwards, looking at the beautiful beach ahead. Imagine that you now draw a line in the sand in front of you. Slowly (or quickly!) in a determined way, step over this line. Start to walk forwards, leaving those painful experiences behind, letting go of all the feelings you had towards them and walking your own path, into your own sunshine, your own Light. Feel the lightness in your body.

Enjoy being in this space of new-found freedom within for a moment, really feeling and breathing in a sense of lightness within. When you are ready, bringing your awareness back to the room that you're in, back to your body. Then taking a couple of deeper breaths, open your eyes, coming back to your meditation space.

Again, I would encourage you to write down, draw and reflect on your experience of the visualisation. There can often be a sense of relief and a letting go of painful feelings during this practice.

If you have been left with residual feelings, you may wish to try the visualisation again or alternatively, you may feel it helpful to seek some support in this.

The visualisation includes a moment of breathing in a sense of *lightness* within and this is another practice I would encourage you to implement from now and as you continue through this book to help you start to embody and to sustain your awareness of your Light.

Being the Light that you are means heightening and sustaining your awareness of this in each moment so that you are able to reach a point when you begin to communicate from this place. Imagine opening your mouth and allowing Divine communication to simply flow!

Donna Collins

This may seem impossible; however, I recall a moment which happened not long after my awakening. I attended a service in a spiritualist church as I was interested to see how experienced mediums worked.

I remember sitting in the congregation and after the medium had addressed another person sitting near to me, I suddenly started to feel tremendous heat through my body and energy on my face, which I experienced like walking into a cobweb. It was like an intense tickling feeling, especially on my nose which no amount of itching would stop!

Unsurprisingly, the medium then addressed me. Her first question was 'Why aren't you standing up here doing this?!' My response was 'because I'm not ready.' The medium smiled and said, 'you're making it too complicated by thinking too much. All you have to do is open your mouth!'

I wasn't ready to stand up as a medium then as my own self-doubt didn't allow me to; however, in time I learnt to trust that this was indeed possible.

I learnt that all we have to do is align ourselves with our hearts and our Light within. We can begin to do this by starting to focus on our breath in each day.

Light breathing technique

Practising our awareness of our breath helps when we can visualise that with every breath, we are not just breathing in air that sustains our physical body, but we are also breathing in our energetic body, our Light, which also nurtures our soul. We can imagine that the action of breathing is a means of integrating our physical body and our spiritual essence.

> Start again by sitting in a comfortable position, closing your eyes and taking your attention within, noticing where this is for you. Bring your attention to your breath, breathing right down into your stomach.
>
> Now imagine that every time you breathe in, you breathe in a beautiful pure white Light. Imagine this Light flowing down through your nose, down your throat, into your lungs. Imagine it is a pure, cleansing and healing Light, sensed through the body like the experience of tasting menthol, clearing your airways, enlivening your lungs and your mind and refreshing your body, now flowing and expanding throughout your entire being.
>
> This is your Light, your Spirit; feel into this Light, feel the sense of freedom and joy this brings.
>
> As you breathe this Light in, imagine breathing out anything that is of a denser frequency that does not resonate with this Light.

Stay in this place for a few moments or minutes until you feel the sense of nurturing of your being that this Light brings.

When you are ready, taking a couple of deeper breaths, bring your awareness back into the room and into your body and open your eyes when you are ready.

As you continue to practise this, it is possible to develop awareness of the presence of your Light in each moment, simply by focusing on your breath, without doing a specific visualisation.

This will reflect your growing awareness of all that you are and heighten your sense of Faith in each day.

In order to *live each day as the Light that you are* I encourage you to nurture these Light frequencies, which we can imagine as Rainbow colours in your heart:

Rainbow Practices

1. Practise the Listening to your Heart breathing technique

2. Practise the Tree visualisation to experience your own Light within

3. Recognise that others have also forgotten who they are

4. Practise forgiveness through understanding, compassion and acceptance

5. Practise the Beach visualisation

6. Practise the Light breathing technique

Chapter Two

Ego Consciousness

———

To begin to understand the human psyche, we can consider an analogy of a baby elephant…

This may raise questions and potentially an eyebrow for you, as a baby elephant's experience may seem far removed from human experience. However, in terms of understanding how the mind or psyche may be fooled into believing things about itself, let's start here.

When an elephant is young, in some countries a rope is placed round its neck in order to start training the elephant to believe things about itself so that it can be controlled by humans.

The young elephant is led around by a person holding the rope, and because the elephant is so small, it is not strong enough to pull away and go in its own direction.

The elephant learns that it is not strong enough to go anywhere other than where it is being led. What is striking about this is that even when the elephant is fully grown and able to pull over an entire tree that it may be tied to, the elephant continues in the belief that it is not strong enough and allows itself to be controlled.

This is what happens to human beings. Given enough experiences with messages about ourselves, we begin to believe we are not strong enough or clever enough. This expands to become the belief that potentially anything about ourselves is not enough. We reject these parts of ourselves and with that we also lose sight of some of our qualities and we stop being all that we are.

Human beings also add to this by taking the messages they receive from other people – given through inappropriate, unnecessary words and actions, especially in childhood – as a direct reflection of who they are as a person. In short, they blame themselves. The harsh, critical voices a person hears become an integrated voice that an individual then uses to berate themself with. The challenge with this scenario is because it is so subtle, we don't know we are doing it, until it stops. This is potentially carried for a lifetime, unless spiritual unfoldment or long-term psychotherapy takes place.

Then begins the next challenge. The ego mind's job is survival, continuously creating a sense of separateness in order to differentiate between Self and others. It also creates constancy and fears change, so stopping the critical voice and belief about the self is even more challenging. Although it is highly painful to hear such criticism and feel so unworthy, it becomes scary to believe anything different as that involves change.

The psyche works hard to maintain a sense of separateness by comparing itself to others. How many times have you thought someone's better than you, or prettier or richer? This can also happen with positive thoughts such as *I am far more experienced or worldly wise or successful than them.* All of these thoughts ultimately create a sense of separateness: we perceive ourselves as something different to other people or objects. Ultimately, this reduces our awareness of our connectedness to all things, including ourselves.

The psyche uses emotional states to reinforce these beliefs such as fear, jealousy, envy and greed. It also uses desire as a means to attempt to avoid these feelings, all of which becomes a repetitive, draining cycle.

Just like the elephant, the rope around the neck is restrictive, and yet it becomes comforting at the same time. We believe we are not restricted. We believe we are free, even though that involves giving up on all that we truly are and our own path in life. We constantly believe we are a smaller version of ourselves because the ego would have us believe that keeps us safe.

But it does not, it keeps us *small*.

Small in our thoughts, small in our fears, small in our sense of lack in ourselves and others. Small in our perception of the world and small in our beliefs and our Faith in ourselves.

Judgement

This smallness occurs amidst the constant belief of not being good enough and blaming ourselves. The one fundamental factor that sustains these beliefs, and in many ways controls our entire life experience, is continuous judgement of ourselves and others.

We need to acknowledge that this fundamental aspect of being human is happening within ourselves, all of the time. We are constantly judging. This realisation is so important, in order to recognise that at every level we are judging everything about ourselves and the way we function.

We have false beliefs about what is OK and what is not OK. We even believe that we should have certain thoughts and not others, certain feelings and not others. And the reason we believe these things – the reason this is happening at all – comes from a core belief and judgement of what it is OK for us to be and what it is not OK for us to be, that we are, as symbols, Angel or Demon manifest in a physical body.

Donna Collins

This is a crucial concept to understand, and a level of acceptance is first required around the concept that this judgement is within us and is occurring constantly, and for most, it is completely unconscious.

It is also completely draining and exhausting because somewhere within us are all the parts of us that we are judging! They are trying to explain and justify themselves. They are trying to be heard and desperately want to be accepted. In fact, we are so busy being in conflict with ourselves that how on earth could we possibly think about the fact that at a profoundly fundamental level, we are not really any of those things? – that is just what we have been conditioned to think!

The way out of judgement at the highest spiritual level is to go way back, come totally out of our individual life experience and consider that Light, pure Light of awareness, is creative energy that put us on this planet in the first place. This pure Light is complete wholeness. When something is whole, it has no separation; it has no opposites; it has no good and bad, and at the same time it has both, as one.

An analogy to understand this is to consider a coin. A coin does not exist unless it has two sides. Without two sides, it is no longer a coin. Therefore in order to exist as human beings with a sense of wholeness, what is needed is to accept that we are all of the parts of ourselves, both sides as it were. Everything we judge and reject about ourselves is desperate to be loved and when we do this, we can become all that we are, which is ultimately Light.

Going Back to Ourselves practice

A powerful way of reclaiming the parts of ourselves that we have rejected is to visualise going *back to ourselves*.

> Start by sitting comfortably in your meditation space that you have created for yourself. Close your eyes and take your attention within. Focus on your breath, breathing right down into your stomach.
>
> Imagine yourself as a child. Really notice what your child is like, not just how they look but also how they are as a young person in the world and their challenges as well as their qualities – perhaps the child that you learnt it was not OK to be.
>
> Now imagine your adult self sitting down next to the child. Look into the child's eyes and say with Love, 'I've come back for you.'
>
> You may feel emotion and that is OK. Now imagine holding the child's hand and hug them if that feels right for you. Really focus on taking this child with you into the present with love. Reassure your child that you are not leaving them again.

When you feel comfortable that your child is now with you, without rejection, without discomfort, take a couple of deeper breaths, bringing your attention back into the room that you are in and back into your body, opening your eyes.

This visualisation can be a very powerful means of experiencing just how much you have rejected yourself. It can bring a lot of emotion, which is totally normal. It is the start of you learning to Love all of you, what you perceive as good and bad. You are learning to remember that regardless of your perception, every aspect of you has been created by the Divine, the Light of Creation itself.

I again would encourage you to write down in your journal your experience and draw what you saw or what you imagine you might have seen if you choose not to do the visualisation.

The pure Light of creation, consciousness in its original form, is dark. Speaking from my experience, it is felt as 'nothing', and this is an experience that has been shared by many on the spiritual path. From this 'nothing', this receptive, dark, feminine or yin energy is born matter, physical form, also known as masculine or yang energy, which we can also see as light.

Physicists describe the 'big bang' theory as if it were a one-off event. In my experience of the dark continuously manifesting light of matter or physical form, I would suggest an alternative concept of continuous 'bangs' or manifesting of light. This is perhaps why scientists have found that the multiverse is constantly expanding and growing and we, as conscious manifestations of Light, are part of it.

This knowing comes from a powerful vision I had years ago when I started to see intense light and colour. The experience was as if I was inside the womb – I could see Light shining through the walls of the stomach, just like if you have ever shone a torch on your hand.

The light was shining through the red of the skin and yet there was also darkness; the darkness in some way provided the energy for the light to appear and when it did that, the space I was in provided me with enough physical light to see and enough air for me to breathe and this was happening through a repeating vibration, a magnitude of sound I had never experienced in the physical, which I knew in the vision was Divine creative light within the darkness. With every pulsing, vibrating sound or 'bangs', Light or physical matter was created.

I have also experienced this regularly during my awakening as an experience of seeing energetic rainfall both outside and indoors – regular visions of the Light of Creation literally creating matter in front of my eyes!

Donna Collins

Try to imagine that this pure light manifests in the human body for a reason, and that reason is to be a vehicle to experience Light in many different energetic frequencies, which we can imagine as colours. These frequencies are just that – different frequencies, different colours. We can call this the Rainbow of Light.

It's incredible to imagine that the originating source can be seen as dark and formless as well as light and of form. This is the very thing that filters through into human life at every level. Our ultimate fears are that we are nothing, simply pure awareness, and we focus on being 'something' which is a physical form. In effect, we are frightened to acknowledge or reveal our source, our own nature, because if we do, we might not survive. What we don't realise is that if we do allow our true nature, our Light, to come to the fore, it is totally reassuring.

We can observe this in people who busy themselves in life trying to prove themselves through things like work or academia, those who will always tell you they are busy. If there is nothing to do, they will find something because it is a way to prevent them from *being* the Light that they are.

At every level we are defended against the dark. The dark brings our ultimate fears to the surface in everything we perceive, with death being the ultimate fear, the fear of being nothing. And yet, spiritually we are eternally conscious at the same time.

These fears filter into every concept imaginable – our fears of being alive or dead, being a man or a woman, masculine or feminine, rich or poor. Ultimately, we start to believe one is good and the other is bad. The good we accept and the opposing perceived bad aspect we don't accept.

These opposites effect how we see the world, other people and our unconscious beliefs about ourselves.

What we have learnt in order to defend ourselves from this ultimate fear is to judge, at every level of human existence.

This is the very fear I observed culturally and socially prior to writing this book – fear of our own Light, our own eternal formless beauty, the Light of Creation, which we can also experience as dark.

The path to wholeness is to recognise that we are all things and at the same time nothing at all. We have the capacity to feel all frequencies and in that we are both Angel and Demon. We experience Love and Hate and this is OK because at the same time, we are neither. Those are just concepts formed out of judgement.

Donna Collins

What makes us who we are is how we choose to act towards ourselves and others, to recognise that sometimes we have thoughts and feelings that are different, that some may label as 'devilish' or 'bad', and that is OK. We can consciously choose to recognise that this is actually what it is to be human – to have an inner world of thought and feelings and to consciously choose what we do about them, which may in many instances, be nothing other than to have a wry smile of 'I know that'.

The key is to recognise that it is our own judgements about ourselves which cause our own desperation to be the Angel, in order to be accepted and to overcome the ultimate fear of the dark. Whereas in actual fact, consider for a moment, how do you know the Angel if you don't know the Demon?

We are here on this earth to experience contrasts, so that we know them. At a soul level, we are here to experience every facet of every emotion, felt through the body, yet we are busy, so very busy, trying not to!

When this concept is fully recognised and experienced, it can bring overwhelming joy. In fact, it can become hilariously funny in some ways once we start to realise that the Angel and Demon, our assumed right and wrong ways of thinking and feeling, are simply illusions. They are concepts made from conditioning, from our experience of others on every level – from the individual to the collective, cultural and societal, implicit conditioning of what is and what isn't acceptable.

Freedom breathing technique

Sit again in your meditation space, close your eyes and take your attention within. Breathe down into your stomach.

Enjoy simply breathing – take a few moments to breathe – breathe in freedom and breathe out restriction. Breathe in hope and Faith and all that you are, and breathe out everything you believe you should be, ought to be, and shouldn't be.

Then focus on practising accepting that you are all things, because that is what you are here to experience. Breathe in acceptance, breathe out conditioning.

When you are ready and have enjoyed staying in this space, bring your attention back to the room that you're in, back to your body, taking a couple of deeper breaths and opening your eyes.

Breathe a sigh of relief. The challenge is then to maintain this level of awareness and acceptance. When thoughts come into your mind and feelings you deem unacceptable, say to yourself, 'Of course I will feel that and think that sometimes. I'm free to choose how I respond. I can laugh at a thought. I am free to experience anything in my inner world without judgement and without labelling myself as anything other than a human being having an experience.'

Another way of checking whether the judgement is continuing inwardly without any level of consciousness is to ask yourself *How much am I judging others?* Notice how you respond when you hear someone saying something you don't necessarily think, or doing something you wouldn't do. Do you understand that they are also on their own path, their own journey towards their own Light and their own experience of wholeness? Do you have compassion for them?

Once you start doing this, you will also start to observe how others also judge you, and this will show you just how much they are judging themselves too!

From judgement to Wisdom

In an attempt to make themselves feel less small and temporarily give some relief and help increase confidence, some may begin intellectualising and reminding themselves of all the things they have achieved in their lives and the number of friends and family that love and value them. This may bring a temporary sense of calm; however, the only way to bring change is to start to experience yourself for all that you are.

The only way to Wisdom is through experience. Knowledge can be acquired in a book such as this, whereas true Wisdom is only found through experience.

So how do we get it?

Firstly, we accept the concept that there is a possibility that we may have forgotten who we truly are. Secondly, we have a willingness to remember, and to do this we need to find the courage to shift our focus from looking externally at all of the distractions we have created for ourselves to looking within for the answer.

We can start to practise personal responsibility. We can stop blaming others for how we feel and start to turn our attention inwards towards our own hearts.

We can also start by learning to understand that the ego mind, by helping us to survive, also restricts us through judgement. It keeps us safe but small, constant but confined, separate but limited.

Donna Collins

Rather than focusing on our smallness and separateness, we can begin to contemplate concepts such as those contained in the following question:

How do we bring the stars down from the sky?

We recognise that they are within us.

You may answer with another question: How can stars possibly be within me?

This would be the psyche's means of limiting your belief about yourself.

Put simply, once we recognise that stars are made from exactly the same thing as human beings at a subatomic level, and that the experience of seeing a star only happens within your own body, we can see that we are not separate to that which we are looking at. In fact, we are the very thing we are looking at.

When we can start to view the world, the multiverse, at this level, we start to see that we are not so separate from the multiverse after all. We are made from the same source, the same creative light. We start to see that it is the psyche that constantly feeds us the information that we are different to, opposite to, the object or person we are looking at or hearing about.

It may be difficult to take in this knowledge and fully embody it at this stage. I remember really struggling to imagine what this might be like when I heard people describe this kind of experience to me. However, I would encourage you to simply practise trying to remain open in your heart and with your mind.

It is possible to start having an embodied experience of what I am describing and often this happens spontaneously, once there is a willingness and an openness. I once had an experience of this when I was on a silent retreat, which I thoroughly recommend as a means of quieting the mind.

Several days into the retreat, I stood outside for some fresh air. My senses appeared heightened as I was taken aback by the beauty of the flowers in the garden; the sun was like pure warm honey on my skin and the breeze was an exquisite, gentle nurturing sensation against my cheeks.

I was completely in the moment. There were no thoughts stirring through my brain, no sense of time, only a presence, my presence, my awareness that felt expanded into a oneness with everything I was observing through my senses. I felt truly alive to all that was.

As I breathed in this heightened sense of beauty, a bee flew towards me and appeared to hover in front of me for what felt like a prolonged moment of stillness and silence. I did not go into thought and label it as a *bee*; I simply viewed it, took it into me and instead of an experience of looking at something outside of myself, I had a profound experience of looking at myself. I felt the bee. At the deepest level of existence, we were the same. I found myself instantly bursting into laughter as I observed the bee. I exclaimed out loud, 'That's me!'

This was a naturally flowing, spontaneous, and what some would describe as mystical experience of simply existing beyond the ego mind and becoming nature itself, and it was joyous! It was an experience I will never forget as a moment of complete aliveness and presence.

This experience can be practised by first opening your mind to the possibility and questioning your current restricted beliefs and perceptions.

For example, try standing and looking up at the sky. Where do you think the sky stops? Your mind will have you believe it is separate, somewhere up near the clouds but in actual fact, you are standing in it, part of it.

It is also possible to overcome this continuing perception of separateness by utilising other practices, such as constantly reminding ourselves to look for similarities. By doing this we are no longer reinforcing separateness that takes us away from our Light; instead we can reinforce unity in every moment.

The next time you find yourself comparing, consider what you have in common with the other person, or object. In terms of people, are you not both human beings with a level of conscious awareness?

How would it be to consider the possibility that the very same consciousness is shared by both of you, part of you both? Part of the very same sky you both imagine to be separate from?

Together with this, it is important to remember that the reason we have forgotten all that we are is that we are all defended against our ultimate fears. We have all identified with our experiences, our thoughts, our psyche and the emotional response it creates, and come to believe that this is the extent of our being.

How is it to imagine that we are not what we have experienced? This can be a very challenging concept for many. This concept is not to belittle in any way our feelings about the experiences – they are valid. However, identifying with the experience and feeling ultimately limits us.

Donna Collins

Treat your ego psyche as your friend

To change this, it is also necessary to learn to treat your ego psyche as your friend. This may feel contradictory, but ultimately to reduce the power our minds have over us and reduce the amount of energy we exert in trying to keep aspects of our psyche quiet, we must learn to love and accept it instead. This means learning to love and accept ourselves, for all that we are. The more accepting of ourselves we are, the less we need to be our false self.

This may sound cheesy for some. Maybe you've heard it all before. What I'm talking about here is not just repeating affirmations in the mirror each day saying, 'I love me.' I'm talking about fully embodying and living the Love that we are.

I often help clients understand this more simply by sharing the concept that *no one can swim with a foot on their head.* What I mean is that whilst we berate and criticise ourselves, we simply cannot be ourselves, we cannot be in the flow of life. So, in simple terms, practise talking to yourself in a different way. The way we speak to ourselves is a direct reflection of how the psyche is functioning. So if you change the words, you have a direct effect on how your mind functions and experiences yourself.

Befriending the ego practice

Every time you criticise yourself, change it to *It's understandable that I feel this way or think this way.*

Remember, acceptance reduces the power the psyche has over us.

Without acceptance, the psyche can literally churn out in every moment an entire sea of words that can keep us literally struggling to tread water, battling with a constant flow of words that take us into the fear of drowning under our own emotional response.

Awareness that, at the ultimate spiritual level, thoughts are a product of fear of our own Light and another means of distraction from who we really are can really help to shift our perspective. Instead, it is possible to meet thoughts with a wise acknowledgement of *I know why you're here. You're here because you're afraid of being all that you are.*

Donna Collins

Simple breathing technique

In that moment of reassuring yourself, it is possible to do that one simple thing: breathe. Simple, yet hugely challenging at times of experiencing an intense emotional response. However, focusing on the breath allows you a momentary space to be in the experience of oxygen flowing in through your nostrils and down into your lungs, shifting your awareness into yourself, your own being.

Focus on the detail of your breath, including the air that touches your nostrils. Notice that the air on the way in is cooler than the air on the way out because it has been warmed through your body. Have you ever taken the time to notice this? Notice what happens when you distract your mind and place your conscious awareness onto something else.

The previous thoughts and feelings, albeit temporarily, stop. Nothing has changed in your external world and yet, in a moment, you can start to feel better.

Focusing on your body helps to override the psyche's focus on thought. Put simply, you cannot be completely in your head if you're in your body. I often ask clients to notice how their toes feel today. Have you taken the time to do this? Your body is just as much 'you' as your head. You are not a head on a stick. Intelligence is within every cell in your physical body as well as your own subtle body, or energetic body.

So notice, how do your toes feel today?

Visualisation: Grounding into the Body

A wonderful visualisation / meditation to help with this is to sit comfortably in a chair, focusing on your breath.

> *Breathe down into your stomach, then gently scan your body for any tension, which is energy stored in specific places. Then focus on breathing out this tension. This will help you learn that you have a conscious choice over how much energy is stored in certain places as long as you practise having awareness of it.*
>
> *Now take your awareness down to your toes. Notice how they feel today. Become aware of the floor supporting your feet, your chair supporting particular places on your body. Gently remind yourself to breathe down into your stomach.*

Staying in this place for a few moments significantly alters your energetic and physical state of being. It takes you out of thought and into your body. It is a practice that takes a few moments and can change how you experience your entire day and life.

By continuing this practice, over time you will start to experience that you are more than the thoughts in your head. This shows you that thoughts take you away from all that you are – beginning with your body and continuing into what some spiritual traditions call the subtle or energetic body, or we can call it your Light.

Most importantly, as you begin, it is key to remember the very first instruction in this book – that you are willingly staying with the concept that you may have forgotten who you are and you are open to remembering.

By doing these practices and staying with these concepts, you are now starting to live your journey towards wholeness and Faith in everyday life.

The following are the Light frequencies I would encourage you to nurture in your heart in order to consciously live with the ego:

Rainbow Practices

1. Gently try the Going Back to Ourselves practice

2. Practise the Freedom breathing technique

3. Practise Befriending the ego on an ongoing basis

4. Practise the Simple breathing technique

5. Practise Grounding into the Body visualisation

Chapter Three

Emotions

In this chapter I interchangeably use the words 'emotion' and 'feelings.' Feelings are generally experienced consciously whereas emotions are experienced both consciously and unconsciously. For the most part, I will use the word *'emotions.'*

Learning to understand emotions is another key aspect of getting to know who you really are.

We can begin by learning that an emotional response can be felt following a present-day experience and also when we consciously remember things that have happened to us.

There are also times when events in the present *trigger* an unconscious emotional response.

A trigger is an unconscious moment in which emotions from childhood and previous painful or traumatic events are experienced in the present day. These emotions tend to be very intense and can motivate a behavioural response that will often appear to be an extreme overreaction to the present-day situation. That is because it is!

It is probable that the unconscious event the person is re-experiencing warrants a more extreme emotional response; however, both the person experiencing it and other people sharing the present-day situation will be completely unaware that is happening.

Having an understanding of this can really help us to increase our self-awareness. It can empower us and encourage us to adopt self-responsibility, and ultimately bring transformation in the way we experience ourselves and our lives.

Healing previous trauma and childhood pain is something we can take responsibility for ourselves. When we really own these aspects of ourselves, we can experience relationships that are without blame.

Understanding triggers helps us to see and accept that *no one makes us feel anything*. Then we can start to choose how we respond to any situation. Yes, other people's actions may not be kind or appropriate and may warrant a response. However, if we can retain our awareness of our own triggers, we can respond in a way that matches the current situation.

Otherwise we may be swept up in a hugely intense emotional response that we feel helpless to consciously choose to process before we take action.

An example of this is when relationships end. The break-up triggers an unconscious emotional response as well as the loss in the present day and individuals can experience this as completely devastating.

It's completely understandable to feel upset during this time. The end of a relationship can feel like a bereavement if our previous partner is no longer in our lives. However, many people are unable to cope with the feelings of rejection and abandonment. They experience intense fear. When this is explored in therapy, it is usually a feeling of *not being able to survive* without this person.

In the majority of cases, what has been triggered is a childhood fear and re-experiencing of abandonment. As young children, we are literally unable to survive without our parents being able to provide us with food and water and so the intense fear felt in adulthood is a re-experiencing of the ultimate possibility of death.

This trigger can happen on an ongoing basis during relationships when things go wrong and we feel like we may *lose* the other person. The unconscious fear of abandonment, how we react to these intense feelings and our behaviour towards our partner can often be the very thing that inadvertently brings the relationship to an end.

The key to happiness in life and the end to a blaming scenario in relationships is to start to recognise the difference between a trigger and a present-day response. Then ask yourself, are you responding to a current situation with feelings that are from the past? Are your feelings about a present situation similar to other events in your life?

Being aware of this concept will help you to become conscious of when *you* may be overreacting.

Emotions and feelings are energy stored, blocked and moving in the body. Knowing this is key to the ability to create a more observational view of what is happening to you. Emotions can be seen literally as energy in motion.

The most common human propensity is to respond to emotions with an action. How many times have you heard someone say, 'That person has upset me, I must "do" something about it.'

It's possible to observe people reacting to this upset by busying themselves with things like housework, often cleaning as a distraction, literally *washing* the pain away or contacting the other person in order to make them see sense.

Donna Collins

The rush to 'do something about it' is actually doing something to ease the difficult emotion that is being experienced. Emotions are challenging to feel in the body and can be very uncomfortable for many people.

There is often a perception that these feelings will go away if something in the external world changes. For instance, if the other person changes their behaviour and apologises or a multitude of other possibilities, such as *if only I could have a holiday, I'll be fine.*

These are the psychic processes which when activated tell us *if I change the external, my internal world will be better. I will feel better.*

However, only **we** can change our inner world, no one else. This includes our emotional responses to the present and our past.

It may sound daunting for us to take responsibility for all of our feelings. However, this can also be totally liberating! How is it to consider for a moment that the intensely difficult feelings you have been struggling to contain all your life can stop having power over you?

The experience of this is something that millions of people are searching for in one form or another – *inner freedom.*

The key here is to start looking within. Separate what is happening in the present, the emotion you are experiencing, and your perception of and reaction to the emotion.

Own it as yours. This is the start of your inner journey towards liberation. It really is as profound as that.

Labelling emotions

A regular experience in my psychotherapy work with clients is to help them let go of labelling emotions as either good or bad, which in turn relates to whether they view themselves as good or bad. I have heard many clients share their perception of anger as something that makes them a 'bad person'.

Many clients have experienced *angry* people in their lives, often as children when their parents have become angry with them. In my experience, this creates an unconscious, young belief that being angry will mean they are like their parent, often perceived as a 'bad person'. Being angry therefore equals being 'bad'.

There is then an unconscious fear of feeling anger.

These fears can be unconsciously directed at any or all emotions, which often means that many people become frightened of feeling anything.

Donna Collins

In therapy the starting point is to help the person differentiate between a behavioural response, so in the case of anger, possible shouting or throwing objects or violence, and the feeling itself.

And to learn that it is OK to feel angry!

When we're feeling angry, it is our chosen behaviour that makes us who we are. Feeling the emotion of anger does not make us a 'bad person.' It makes us a human being!

Changing our perception of all emotions is absolutely necessary if we are to get to the Light within, as whilst emotions are judged there is another reaction within the psyche, which is resistance to the emotion itself; this only intensifies and exacerbates the emotion further.

The starting point for inner emotional freedom is to stop labelling any emotion as good or bad.

Imagining instead our emotions as a spectrum of light, or as termed earlier in this book, a Rainbow of Light, with each emotion having its own beautiful frequency of colour is a very powerful means of learning to accept all emotions as simply energy in motion through the body. By doing this we can let go of identification with the emotions themselves.

This in turn helps us to remember that emotion does not have to equate to action. This is a crucial part of self-awareness as well as being aware that *what you feel is not who and what you are.*

How many times have you found yourself saying, 'I am anxious' or 'I am afraid'? Your words are literally naming how you perceive yourself and what you identify with and believe you are. These statements do not describe the Truth. Truth is another word for Spirit or Light, and as described in the first chapter, Light is never anxious nor afraid nor angry.

Focusing on changing your terminology during these moments is crucial to beginning to experience your emotions and yourself differently.

Re-framing terminology practice

The next time you experience an emotion, for example sadness, try using the following language:

'I am experiencing *sadness* at the moment.' This can be changed to include any emotion you may experience.

This subtle change in language completely changes how you perceive yourself. Described in this way, you are creating an experience that suggests two things:

A) I am something more than the emotion I am experiencing.

B) This emotion will pass.

As well as imagining our emotions as a Rainbow of different Light frequencies and learning to speak differently to ourselves, it is also really important to consciously use our breath in order to help create space for emotions to flow through.

Being conscious of our posture, sitting up straight whilst having our feet on the floor whilst consciously breathing down into the stomach is the start of living a life that does not feel like being a slave to our emotions; ultimately, as stated previously, we can begin to create an experience of space and freedom within.

It is important that for this the intention is 'being with' or 'creating space' for the emotion to flow through rather than trying hard to avoid feeling it by breathing out as forcefully as possible! This is very important as trying to push feelings away has the opposite effect. It literally results in us tightening within, trying to hold on to some sense of control and this exacerbates the feeling instead of creating space for it to flow.

Breathing with Emotions technique

To begin, sit with a good posture, with your back supported, setting the intention of thought that you are going to breathe with the emotion you are experiencing, creating space within to allow it to flow through you so that you can breathe out the emotion.

Close your eyes if you wish or keep your eyes open, gazing gently ahead in a restful position. Focus your attention within your body. Notice where in your body you are experiencing the emotion. As you retain your attention on this place in your body, gently breathe in through your nose, allowing the breath to flow down into your lungs, notice your chest expand and then a little further, allowing your stomach to expand also.

Imagine that you are creating space within for the emotion (the energy in motion) to flow through your body, remembering that this is not going to take over you. You are something more than the emotion, the energy itself, as you have conscious choice to allow the space!

Now focus on breathing out. Allow your stomach to deflate gently followed by your lungs and breathe out of your mouth, visualising breathing the emotion out of the body with Love.

Stay in this space, breathing gently, ensuring you are not breathing in additional air but simply allowing the air you do breathe in to flow down into the stomach.

Continue until you start to feel the emotion subside; let it pass.

When you are ready, bring your awareness back to the room that you're in, back to your body, taking a couple of deeper breaths, opening your eyes or simply bringing your attention to the room around you.

This breathing technique can be used repeatedly, wherever you are; with eyes open, simply notice the emotion in your body and breathe with it. It is a very powerful tool to use in the everyday in order to create space, not just to feel the emotion until it passes but also to continue being conscious enough to choose how you would like to respond to any given situation in a calmer, less emotive way.

To further assist in living consciously with emotions, we can also add a visualisation to the breathing technique that we can do on our own to enhance our ability to allow emotions to flow and dissipate.

Visualisation: River

Imagine that you are sitting by the side of a beautiful river. You are surrounded by nature, hearing the birds tweeting and the breeze blowing softly against your skin.

Imagine that the water flowing along the river is your emotions. The crucial part here is to start to see that you are sitting by the side of the river. You are not in it. This creates a subtle distance in your psyche that says 'I am not the emotion I am experiencing.' The flowing water also allows you to see that this emotion is going to do just that, flow away in front of you; you will not continuously feel it.

Sometimes the water may bring with it a twig or something that gets caught on a rock, which may take more time to flow through and may feel more intense. However, retaining awareness that this will pass in itself helps the water continue to flow through.

Using the Breathing Out Emotions technique above, imagine your breath is the water in the river. Focus on breathing the emotion out, letting it flow through you as well as enjoying the inward breath, which can also help you to fully embody emotions like joy too!

Take a few moments to enjoy being in this place. Notice the energy change within you as you feel more of a free, flowing sensation within.

When you are ready, take a couple of deeper breaths, bringing your awareness back into the room that you're in, back to your body and when you are ready, open your eyes.

This visualisation can be practised repeatedly. This is a wonderful tool to empower you to know that you are not a slave to your emotions. You simply need to provide a space for them to be heard and felt so that they can flow through you more quickly. I would recommend practising the breathing technique regularly so that you can utilise this method on its own as sometimes you may find that it is not possible in certain situations to sit in the quiet with your eyes closed in order to do the visualisation. However, it is always possible to breathe!

In my experience, the more you practise, the shorter the time it takes for emotions to move through and dissipate. It is possible for this to happen in anything from one to a few minutes. This can be very liberating for many people, to be able to re-experience inner space and freedom in a short period of time. It also reduces the number of times we find ourselves reacting in situations and doing things that perhaps we would regret later.

It also helps to re-affirm the sense and knowing that you are something greater than your emotional state.

The ultimate Wisdom through experience here is to be aware that the psyche is very complex and can distort your perception of scenarios and your thoughts and feelings about them. Remembering that at the ultimate spiritual level, this is an attempt by the psyche to retain your beliefs about yourself through fear, which ultimately takes you away from your Light.

Rainbow Practices

1. Practise imagining your emotions as a spectrum of Rainbow of Light, all different frequencies with no 'good' or 'bad'

2. Practise re-framing your terminology regarding your emotions

3. Practise the Breathing with Emotions technique

4. Practise the River visualisation

Chapter Four

Love

---

*Beyond the spectrum of beautiful colour
lies the pure Light that created it,
experienced in the heart space by man as LOVE*

To write a chapter about Love is more challenging than one might imagine, mainly because of the infinite number of words that can be used to describe it that can also, if used incorrectly, undermine the Beauty and intensity of how Love is experienced.

So first, imagine if this chapter was to tell you that Love didn't exist. Many would protest with, 'Of course it does, I've felt it.'

This also applies to every experience deemed spiritual. Spiritual awareness, in the same way as Love, has to be felt through the body, and most would say through the heart predominantly, in order to be believed. And so, the similarity between Love and Spirit begins…

Although we can think about Love, we only really know it when we feel it. Love is a hugely powerful force that has been the motivator for many acts of bravery, courage, war and the search for peace. It is also the inspiration of many songs and creativity.

Love, when thought of as another emotion, can be seen as another colour in the Rainbow of Light with its own frequency. However, this would be an incorrect supposition.

To use a rainbow as an analogy, colour is seen during certain conditions by the human eye. However, that colour is created by something else, the Light from which it came. This is creative Light or energy that manifests in physical form.

Love can be seen as the same creative light as that which creates a rainbow. When certain objects or molecules, like water, get in the way, the pure Light frequency is separated into different colours or frequencies, which include many that the human eye is unable to see.

This is suggestive of the same concept as the sun and its rays. The sun creates and emanates its rays, just as creative

Donna Collins

Light emanates a rainbow – they are one, no beginning and no end, one and the same thing.

How is it to imagine that the Beauty of a rainbow is like seeing inside yourself? You are unable to see clearly what has created it, nor its full range of frequencies. A rainbow is, in fact, a complete circle, simply unseen by the human eye unless you're lucky enough to catch a glimpse from the air.

This tells us two important things. First, Love, the pure Light frequency, is the source of what we are. Secondly, Love gives us the capacity to experience more and more frequencies than we are aware of.

To give more of an understanding of how Love is experienced, we can consider again what happens when relationships come to an end. As well as potential triggers, the other experience that many people have, which you may have experienced or heard someone say, and has certainly been written about, is the experience of *love lost*.

This is a really important concept to explore. It is suggestive of love being given to us by the other and when the relationship ends, love goes too. This creates an intensely painful experience, one of loss, not just of the person, but our very Source.

And sadly, it's not true.

Love does not come from someone else, it comes from within. It is what and who we are.

When we really start to embody this, we can let go of trying to get it from elsewhere. This is a life-changing concept as when we do this, life shifts from a place of 'something is missing' to a sense of complete wholeness and abundance and this in itself is hugely liberating and becomes a profound experience.

No longer do we need to chase relationships that are often not in our best interests in search of Love. No longer do we need to sit in despair believing that we are unlovable because we start to believe and embody truly living the day-to-day experience of being Love itself.

Just as the light of a rainbow is there the whole time, so is the Love that we are. It's simply that often there are clouds, sometimes dark clouds that get in the way. Different conditions such as no rain prevent you from seeing the rainbow; likewise, differing life circumstances affect us and prevent us from being aware of the Love that we are. In fact, it is so hidden in some human experience that often it is as if the sun and blue sky were never there at all, forgotten about or only experienced as tiny, infrequent glimpses.

Donna Collins

These clouds that come in the form of life experience bring feelings about what has happened and who we believe we are, as described in the previous chapter, and ultimately away from Love.

So, how do we start to experience the Love that we are?

Once we are aware that the psyche does a fantastic job of comparing ourselves to others and, often, unconsciously believing that our qualities are solely within others, we can start to consciously choose something different. With this in mind, we can start to see how much of the Love that we are we give to others.

Recognising we are Love does not mean that we don't still feel love for others and others don't love us, it simply means that we can consciously choose to experience something else as well. We can recognise that, regardless of how we feel about other people, Love is always within us.

Visualisation: Experiencing Love within

We can practise experiencing ourselves as Love by thinking about the Love we feel for someone else.

Sit comfortably, breathing down into your stomach and relaxing your body.

Now bring to mind someone or something that you Love. Really focus your attention on the feeling of Love that you have for that person or thing. Now notice where you feel Love in your body. Try gently focusing on breathing that feeling of Love in through your nose and down into your lungs. Fill your lungs with Love, breathing out any impurities. Let Love consume you, imagining Love filling all of your being, flowing down through your arms, into your hands, down into your stomach and your legs, into your feet. Take a moment to enjoy this sensation.

Notice the change within you; you are literally changing the frequency of your entire being, each and every cell, to Love.

Practise this as often as you can – breathing out tension, breathing in Love, like menthol, fresh and rejuvenating. Continue to focus on the sensation of the feeling through your body. You may also see Love as an image or a colour.

Donna Collins

In time, through focusing on this practice, it is possible to start to become aware that Love has within it other qualities, which are initially very subtle and become more vivid, such as Beauty, joy and peace.

We start to experience that the word 'Love' which we use to describe a feeling in our heart space, can also be used to describe the very same qualities as Light. It is possible then to realise that Love and Light are the same thing.

When we continue to use the rainbow as an analogy and the complete circle the rainbow creates, we can also see that the Light is continuous in nature. Like the sun and its rays, they are one, no beginning and no end, which also gives us insight into the nature of Light as infinite, expansive and eternal. This in turn tells us that Love is the same in nature – you are the same.

Experiencing this fully takes practice over time. It involves completely letting go of all the things you've previously identified with before. Using all the tools given in this book, you will start to notice a shift in your inner experience.

Your psyche will try to take you away from the full extent of what you are, and it is important to always remember that it is your psyche's job of survival to ensure this happens to retain your perception that you are a small, isolated, individual being and the fear that you experience will keep you in this place.

So it is essential to remind yourself, 'That is my psyche's resistance to me experiencing all that I am.'

This is constant maintenance. Always.

Ask yourself the Love question

It is also possible when faced with challenges in life, and we need to make a decision, to ask ourselves *What would Love do?*

This is a powerful way of effectively bypassing the ego mind and choosing something which is more in alignment with Light.

When we do this we come away from judgement, we come away from harshness and criticism, we soften, we become more understanding, we open our hearts and we feel compassion and all the other qualities of Light that are stated in this book, and fundamentally, we become happy!

Love brings peace, joy and happiness and also a sense of certainty. Love always knows the answer – it contains Wisdom.

So if, as spiritual beings, we are Love, then ask yourself again, *How many times have I experienced or felt Love today?* And keep asking this.

Rainbow Practices

1. Practise the Experiencing Love Within visualisation

2. Practise challenging your psyche's resistance to being all that you are

3. Practise asking yourself the LOVE question

4. Ask yourself each day, *how many times have I experienced Love (my true Self) today?*

Chapter Five

Creativity

Creativity is the bridge between the physical and the spiritual

When we spend time practising and allowing ourselves to be the Love that we are, not only do we experience a shift within ourselves in terms of our level of happiness, but we start to also experience a constant flow of life force energy. It flows beyond all the self-limiting and distorted beliefs of who we are.

Donna Collins

Imagination practice

Imagine being told today that all of your external constraints in life have been taken away, and all of your difficult relationships have stopped. You are now completely free to simply do what is in your heart to do… Imagine the excitement you would feel. Imagine the joy. Imagine the rush of energy.

Now, stop for a moment and consider what it would be like if, in this moment, you simply started to believe this is the case right now, regardless of any external changes. Imagine instead that, despite anything going on around you, you can simply imagine that you are still free to choose, free to think, free to feel something different. Imagine that if you do this, your external world will start to change too.

It may help you to imagine by writing down all of the feelings you believe you would experience if you were completely free to follow your heart. Imagine that this has happened already and you are doing it. Write down what it feels like now that all of your challenges and restraints in life have gone.

This exercise is something you can do anytime with anything you dream of doing in your life. The universe or God responds to emotions, not thoughts, and it responds at the same frequency and by doing so, it brings you more of the feelings you have asked for.

What is so beautiful about this is that you don't have to know any of the details of how it's going to happen. All you have to do is ask for the feeling, simply by imagining what it will feel like.

Your psyche will probably jump into action right now and you will start to experience all sorts of questions and self-doubt. You will probably experience thoughts such as *how ridiculous, of course I can't just stop paying bills or leave my partner.*

Imagine if your psyche were simply implementing these thoughts in order for you to continue to believe you are a small, helpless, isolated, individual being that has no choice. Why? Because remaining small in some distorted way continues to make you feel safe. Because change is too scary.

In this moment, you will know exactly what your psyche uses as its main defence, as you have just experienced the thoughts in your head. This is great, as you will now be able to name that as your resistance to change, to becoming the Light that you are.

Donna Collins

Instead, what if you allowed yourself to enter into the possibility that, as a concept, it is possible to start to change things for yourself by starting to believe something different, and that this belief in itself is the start of changing your external world?

To begin, you simply go back to the start of this book and accept that you may have forgotten all that you are; you work again through the practices and start to practise often, experiencing the Love that you are until you begin to experience the other subtle qualities within the Love that you feel within.

Creativity is the simple practice of allowing Love, with all its expansive qualities, to flow through the heart, undistorted; for Love and Light is also joy, and since its nature is expansive, it is always looking to grow and evolve. It is only a limiting self-belief, an identification with the psyche's need to be small and separate, that keeps us from being in this continuous flow of energy, and this flow is the energetic flow of life itself. It is possible that life can start to feel like a beautiful flow of energy, like floating downstream.

Love Flowing Through the Heart practice

When we start to experience this, in the only way possible, as energy expanding and flowing through the heart, we can start to experience life in the same way as those 'creative' people who thrive by creating things such as music, art, literature, poetry and anything deemed 'designing'.

This image of creativity, however, is incredibly limiting in itself and is not the full Truth. It is also possible to create something bigger, something even more profound than the most beautiful piece of music ever written. It is possible to create a life that you Love.

By that I mean being in the flow, learning to use Love as our compass, by living in alignment with the Love that we are. But how does this actually manifest in our lives as this is the true essence of *Faith in the everyday*?

When creativity starts to flow, this energy bubbles up into consciousness as an unlimited flow of ideas and endless possibilities about what we would like and are going to do with our lives – every day.

Donna Collins

In fact, I have experienced flowing ideas and passionate possibilities in a never- ending stream over several consecutive days. When this happens, fear does not hold us back; we flow with those ideas that we resonate with the most. When we ground this energy through our bodies, we make things happen and our lives change.

Life changes because we have learnt to listen to another part of ourselves, a part that is creative by nature. We are flowing outside of our conditioned minds which would otherwise limit us by having us believe all the things that keep us small and tell us we can't do things.

In many spiritual traditions there are profound phrases such as:

'As above, so below.'

And:

'On Earth as it is in Heaven.'

This in effect means that our inner and outer experience becomes aligned. 'As above, so below', to me, also means 'as within, so without.'

So following this concept, we create a life we love externally, by being Love internally. Both become aligned.

The symbol of the circle or the sun with its rays shows how these two things merge into one. Neither aspect is separate, both are created by one another.

In the same way, once we begin, we forget the exact moment we started and, as the nature of Love or Light is expansive and infinite, we never stop being Love.

As well as allowing Love to flow through the heart, we can also strengthen our awareness, and alignment with our creativity, by starting to recognise that creativity is also the frequency of joy.

Joy is felt through the body as a feeling similar to an adrenaline rush, like excitement, but rather than being hugely intense then fading, it can be continuously felt, sometimes in a more subtle way, as stated previously, as an aspect of Love. This can sometimes be so subtle that we need to practise feeling into Love to experience its other aspects.

We can also access creativity by really being with the feeling of things that have happened in life that we have experienced wonderment at: the excitement of a child, simply trying something new, the wonder of the world, nature, standing in the rain, riding a bike for the first time, realising you can do something for yourself, your first

Donna Collins

boyfriend or girlfriend or your first kiss or falling in Love – a feeling that anything then is possible, no limitations.

Do you remember that feeling? Can you remember thinking you didn't realise that was possible? When was the last time you felt that? A feeling then of *Well, if I can do that, I can do this. I can become anything I can truly imagine…*

Creativity is going beyond all previous ideas and beliefs of what you are capable of. When it flows, the psyche does not get in the way, so there are no restrictions on the feeling, and in this way it becomes infinite. The heart becomes free to open to joy and Love and continues to expand.

How is it to acknowledge that creativity is not just a feeling, or an experience – it's fundamentally what you are? Love and Light are joyful, expansive and creative, which means there are infinite ways of expressing yourself if you learn to allow it.

Every time a new poem or play or a piece of music is written or a work of art is painted or drawn or sculpted or anything new is designed, this is the Light expressing itself through a human being.

This tells you that creativity is possible for you too! And by that I mean, creatively flowing in your life, creating new experiences, new relationships, new depths of feeling, new joy, anything that you believe is possible, without doubts and what ifs holding you back.

Creativity is endless, meaning it can be applied to all aspects of life, like gardening or making your bed or the type of relationship you're in, and it includes how you choose to perceive the world. The key is to recognise that you are the designer of your own life, how you would like to feel in it and what you choose to experience.

Creativity naturally flows through every human being on this planet. What stops it from happening is fear – fear of your own Light, fear of standing above the crowd, fear of being seen for all that you are.

Because the psyche is also afraid of change, it learns to keep itself small, just like the elephant. The heart becomes closed and closes to Love and its beautiful capacity to create.

Donna Collins

Visualisation: Wonderment

Imagine being a child and seeing the world for the first time. Imagine the wonderment that would be experienced. Perhaps you remember this yourself or have seen it in the eyes of a young baby. This is also a way to access creativity, as well as experiencing the Beauty within yourself.

Beauty is also an aspect of Love and Light, so a means of accessing the same frequency of joy and creativity is to remember just how much of a miracle you are, and the planet you live on is, in this majestic universe.

When you take time to observe the world around you, you start to notice how other creatures and nature simply are that. They don't sit around feeling apathetic or bored or lonely. They simply are present in the world.

Practising this presence in the moment is another means of accessing this frequency because it again brings you out of your thoughts and ego consciousness into a sense of connection with something greater.

I have often observed this sense of presence in creatures that 'busy' themselves. I spent many moments contemplating what it was about the busyness of creatures such as squirrels and bees that captivated me so much until one day I realised that they are the epitome of *aliveness,* which is ultimately being completely present in the moment.

Squirrels and bees are not sitting worrying about the next bill they need to pay or comparing themselves to other creatures. They are simply being all that they are and all they were put on this planet to be.

Imagine having this experience, every day.

When was the last time you allowed yourself to draw a picture or paint one, or have fun making patterns out of stones? Or even allowed yourself to sing at the top of your voice?!

How much are you limiting yourself and holding your creativity back from designing a life that you Love? This is ultimately holding yourself back, not just from *doing* but from *being* all that you are.

You can use your answer to the last question as a gauge to how closed your heart is and also how afraid you are of your own greatness. This is normal. You are not alone in this. You can also choose something different in this very moment.

Visualisation: Deer Encounter

This is a beautiful practice for being in the moment and experiencing the wonderment of nature.

> Close your eyes and take your attention within. Notice where 'within' is for you. This can be different for everyone. There is no right or wrong. Focus on your breath, breathing down into your stomach.
>
> Now imagine that you are walking through crisp, white, untouched snow on a beautiful winter's day. The air is fresh and cool around you, and although it is cold, you are wearing beautifully warm and nurturing clothes so that you can enjoy your experience completely.
>
> You feel completely alive with the freshness of the air and the clear blue sky with the sun shining down on the fresh, white snow. You feel the warmth of this on your face.
>
> You walk towards a wood ahead of you. As you approach the trees you notice the Beauty of the white frost on the branches. In that moment you hear a sound and look ahead of the initial trees. There you see a deer. The deer looks back at you; you are encountering each other.

You notice the breath of the deer meeting the cold air and gentle waves of frosty breath form in the atmosphere.

There is a moment during the encounter when you and the deer are connected so strongly in awareness that it is just the two of you on the entire planet, and the world stops. Its eyes, so beautifully deep and clear in their brownness, draw you in. You are unable to move. No thoughts enter your head; you simply experience the wonderment and aliveness of being face to face, eye to eye, being to being. Two beings in the canvas of life, on the whole planet, in the entire universe…

Practise continuing to be in this moment of wonderment. Breathe, breathe with the deer as one.

When you are ready, take a couple of deeper breaths, bringing your awareness back into your body, back to the room that you are in and when you are ready, open your eyes.

This practice can be a hugely effective and beautiful means of being present. This is particularly powerful once you realise that life itself can be experienced in the same way as looking into the eyes of an incredibly beautiful deer.

This is because it is a two-way process, affected by both perception and experience. One creates the other. Looking at the deer causes appreciation of Beauty and a wonderment of life. Likewise, experiencing an appreciation of Beauty and a wonderment of life through practice, creates our perception of things in life as beautiful and to be wondered at.

In effect, you are the deer, which, when truly realised and embodied, is a deeply profound, life-changing experience.

By this I mean that when looking into the eyes of the deer, for many people, they experience wonderment at the sheer beauty and presence looking back at them. They may also feel connection and Love. The deer is a symbol, an image that helps you get in touch with these feelings. We can't feel these things unless they are within us – this means this is you!

You are experiencing your true nature, which is perfection. It can be felt as serene calmness, stillness, purity and beauty, looking right back at you in the form of a deer, without the judgement you place on yourself to be anything more than you already are.

The key to maintaining this perception, as well as the other practices encouraged in this book, is to continuously remind ourselves of the gift of life and to practise gratitude, which will be discussed further in a following chapter.

Faith in Everyday Life | Creativity

Rainbow Practices

1. Practise the Imagination visualisation

2. Practise allowing Love to Flow Through Your Heart

3. Practise the Wonderment visualisation

4. Practise the Deer Encounter visualisation

Chapter Six

Surrender Through the Heart – Learning to be Humble

The following poem flowed through my heart during a meditation and yoga session. I experienced a vision of myself kneeling down in a meadow full of flowers, my head lower than every petal, and I was overwhelmed by the experience of Love and the Beauty of Light.

i am a flower amongst flowers
A blade of grass in a meadow
A grain of sand in a desert
A tiny being amongst beings
An atom in the multiverse
Bowing my head to the experience of the humility
Of the huge power and Grace of God's Love
You give me life, breath and consciousness
To have this awareness of myself
Enough that i never feel greater than

Anyone or anything
And in this humility
I can shine
Brighter than the brightest star
Greater than the most powerful Light
Humbleness giveth Light
And Light itself is Love
The more i surrender
The more I become
One with the greatest power
One with the greatest Wisdom
An eternal Light and Loving flame

The most striking aspect to me of this incredible experience was to feel for the first time the true magnificence of God. In this moment, I experienced the most overwhelming, ecstatic, and at the same time, subtly gentle, serene presence of Light, and with it, something else: humbleness.

Even as I write this, in order to help others, I am overcome with emotion.

This is the hardest and yet the most beautifully fulfilling experience that some who are committed to the spiritual path will be blessed to experience.

Donna Collins

The poem itself depicts the experience, starting intentionally with a lowercase 'i' and as I lower myself in line with other flowers, my perspective of who 'i' am changes. As 'i' bow, the 'I' within me becomes known.

This may seem contradictory; however, this experience comes when lowering the ego's sense of importance and a need to 'do' and to 'prove' makes way for the soul, for God consciousness to be felt and lived in each day.

The colourful energetic frequencies, the Rainbow of Light that starts to be felt along the spiritual journey, become more and more subtle the more sensitive an individual becomes. The absolute key to spiritual unfoldment is to learn the subtlety of 'allowing'.

This happens through a developed sense of humility. Humbleness is the path to truly experiencing magnificence and glory.

This may sound for some a little over dramatic, but ultimately the true Self or Light is magnificent and glorious as well as humble, amongst all the other qualities in the Light we have already discussed.

Awareness of magnificence and glory takes longer to experience through the heart as it requires a deepening of Wisdom and a true embodiment of Faith or Light in order for this to happen, and, as I have described, it is possible to experience spontaneously when a person is ready.

The spontaneity of humbleness can also occur through something happening in life that can feel so overwhelming, for example a bereavement, as well as other life experiences such as the feelings of powerlessness experienced in relationships or if something happens in life that brings an immense feeling of injustice, for example someone being injured by another.

Any experience that invokes such an intense emotional response and feeling of helplessness that, to use an analogy, we have no choice but to *lay down arms* and surrender.

I refer to this type of experience as one of being h*umbled*. It is as if we have no choice but to *bow down* to something far more powerful than ourselves. And it is at this very moment that God can enter us, in all our pain and suffering; in our *giving in* we can find a sense of greatness, an inner strength that cannot be broken.

On the spiritual path, this humbling can happen numerous times and can often last for prolonged periods of time that can bring a sense of impending doom. This is also a humbling of the ego. It is known by those who have been through it as 'the dark night of the soul'.

It is crucial to be aware of this if you are traversing a spiritual path as many people stumble (literally) into this and feel they have somehow lost their way. This experience is, again, an intense humbling of the ego in order to experience the spirit and is firmly part of the path rather than being lost.

If you do experience this, I would advocate finding support from friends and others that are on the spiritual path as it can feel very overwhelming.

Aside from this type of experience however, it is also possible to experience magnificence and glory through practising humbleness. This may sound like a contradiction because it really is that!

This again is because it is a practice of learning to 'get out of the way' of and not preventing the experience from happening.

It may help to understand this more by seeing it as something similar to the experience of trying hard to hold sand in your hands. Initially, the ego wants to hold as much as possible. There is a desperate attempt to dig into the sand and fill each hand with as many grains as you can. And yet, no matter how hard you try, it simply flows through your fingers, causing frustration and disappointment. The more you hold on to, the more the grains fall back into the sand beneath you. However, if you stop trying and simply stay still, with your upturned palms relaxed, you will look into your cupped palms and see that you still have some grains. Because you have stopped trying so hard, you have stopped succumbing to greed or desire and you have simply become accepting and allowing of what remains in your hands.

Rather than focusing on what your psyche perceives it is lacking – fewer grains than it believed it should hold – it is possible to start to feel the Beauty of what you *do* hold, and to see that within each grain is the entire desert. You simply didn't realise it.

When this realisation happens, it is like crystal clear spring water, reflecting the sun's rays. The full power of the sun is felt because it is completely undistorted; it is a pure reflection of the sun in all its glory.

This experience brings clarity, a sense of hope, fulfilment and at the same time a feeling of being home. Nothing to be done, no more seeking to gain. It can also feel overwhelming as the power of Beauty is indescribable.

This wordless, formless Beauty, which holds within it Love and Creativity, is the full extent of your being, the Truth of who you are.

Donna Collins

This is the ultimate contradiction in life and is very difficult to digest in a culture which constantly promotes *doing* and striving for *things* in order to *be* someone.

It is a controversial concept to start to believe that the opposite is true. When we start allowing ourselves to be all that we are, we start being the Light that we are, then we start becoming the Creativity that we are.

Many people respond to this by going into what is termed 'black and white' thinking. This is the psyche trying again to defend against the ultimate truth that it does not exist as a singular, isolated being, and because of this does not ultimately control its existence and environment. The thought process goes something like *I can't possibly just stop doing everything and live in some sort of 'airy fairy' way without any sense of purpose.*

I am not suggesting doing nothing. Being your true nature does not mean being completely still physically and stagnating. It does not mean turning your hands over and tipping all of the sand away. It means allowing your creativity and expansive nature to flow into ideas and experiences that resonate with this.

Many people respond again here with fear as in, 'Yes I see but I have to earn money to live.'

And I agree, money is an essential part of a happy life. What I am describing here is simply acquiring money in a different way.

One way is to act from a place of fear and lack – 'I have to pay my mortgage' – and spending hours trying to work out how, using some form of rational thought, which inevitably takes you away from your true being.

The alternative is to practise allowing yourself to be all that you are; use this frequency as a gauge to inform you of what resonates with you and follow this creativity. Some acts of creativity will happen to generate money.

How would it be to spend all of your time in alignment with who you are instead of following a limiting mentality which incorporates thought processes such as *It's a means to an end. I do this so I can do things that I enjoy or so I can LIVE my LIFE.*

This is a myth, a false belief that has been passed down from generation to generation for literally thousands of years.

When we think of life, our sheer existence on this planet as well as the planet itself and everything on it, within it and around it, as energy, we can start to see that our very thoughts, which are energetic frequencies, create the world

Donna Collins

in which we live, even the ones that say *If I always work hard, I will get the things I want...* This very thought simply creates hard work... and how do we really know what we want if we are not actually being our true selves?

Being humble does not mean being weak or being still; it means listening to yourself in a different way, in a state of Faith that you are more than you believe you are. To make an analogy, this means that rather than thinking you know where you should be heading in your motor boat to one particular point on the opposite side of the bank, you learn to realise that the journey is just as important, so you take a sailboat instead and learn to trust that just maybe the wind knows something more than you do and you may well end up somewhere more beautiful.

The motor boat is the ego, exerting desire to get where it wants to go. The sail-boat is learning the subtlety of the soul, the wind, the feeling, the felt sense in your body that guides you.

I have seen this many times in psychotherapy sessions with clients who are experiencing difficulties in life trying to achieve the goals they have set for themselves. This seems particularly prevalent in a corporate environment.

One particular client had always set himself specific goals of achievement at work, only to find that when he did make those things happen, symbolically, driving his boat to where he thought he should go, he felt a real sense of disappointment and sadness. He had not realised that by aiming at one thing, he was actually limiting himself.

This was because his idea of what would make him happy, the amount of money he would earn, never filled the void that was within him; it never filled his sense of inadequacy as this was a deep-rooted belief in himself that had to be healed within him first. It meant that no matter how much he achieved at work, he didn't feel any better about himself.

His therapy was therefore about learning to be in a sail-boat instead, listening to his heart's desires, learning his soul purpose and what made him feel really alive inside. He started to embody the importance of experiencing and enjoying his life instead, the beauty and sense of connection with nature, which in turn was connecting with himself, his own true nature.

This had a profound effect on this client's life. He started to relax; he no longer felt as much inner pressure on himself to do more, to be more, and he started to feel happy. He shared experiencing joy in the everyday and felt more confident. The change in how he felt about himself improved his relationships with those close to him and with his work colleagues as he felt more authentic and able to be more open and at ease with himself.

His inner peace then gave him space to follow what he was drawn to in his heart and he started doing new things in life – reading new books, getting a dog, and opening his heart to the possibility of a change in career altogether.

And so, when the subtle act of being a *sail-boat* is practised and realised, something profound happens. Our bodies, through the heart space, start to communicate with us in a way we never knew we could listen.

We start to use this feeling, this sense of our innate frequency, as our compass, and we learn to listen to our inner knowing that tells us if the things we have chosen in our lives are in alignment with what some call our soul purpose, the very reason we are here on this planet.

Being humble is also the ability to say 'I don't know', and to know it's OK in this moment. Realistically, our thoughts can't possibly know everything because we are limited to our experience, or to reading about things in books, which gives us *some* knowledge, but true Wisdom can only be gained through experience, and this is what the soul is here for.

Consider for a moment, how many things in your life right now do you feel are a chore? What things would you stop or put down right now if you could? Imagine these things, whatever they may be, as spinning plates. For example, they could be your job, your friendships, your hobbies – anything.

Consider why you started them and why you are continuing doing them.

Now start to see that each spinning plate takes your energy to ensure it keeps spinning. I imagine that fear motivates you to spend your life spinning a chore-like plate! So how would it be to simply stop? Then the fear comes when we consider *what if that happens?* The plate might smash... and... so what?!

Your fears created the thought to start spinning. Your fear motivated you to continue. So by stopping spinning what you are really now saying is, 'I'm choosing to not live in fear any more.'

Your psyche, your ego consciousness, the one that struggles to be humble, has created your world. Letting go first means stopping spinning, stopping being afraid, and instead trusting that there is something greater within you that comes from a deeper place of Wisdom, and that Wisdom comes through your heart. Trust that by stopping expending all of your energy on spinning plates that you don't want, you can create space to allow your energy to flow elsewhere.

When you allow this to happen, you become greater than you have ever imagined because your soul or spiritual essence or God consciousness knows no fear, as it is Light, which as you now know is Love.

Donna Collins

Humility is the path towards knowing your true Light. It is far more subtle than the act of kneeling, although this physical act shows what is necessary within.

This subtle surrendering brings a shift in the way you live your life. It can often bring huge relief, to realise that the mind is not holding the key to everything in the existence of the universe. That is a huge weight off!

When the term 'God consciousness' is used, it is the understanding that consciousness is not created by the brain. Consciousness is within every atom in the multiverse. Pioneers of quantum physics discovered the *observer effect*. This essentially refers to the concept that within each atom is a wave of possibilities. Particles within the atom only become a specific point when it is observed consciously. We can draw from this that atoms have intelligence. This is what pure consciousness is and this can also be described using the word 'God'.

We are made of the very same atoms. Within us is also an infinite 'wave' of possibilities, affected by our consciousness, our thoughts, which in turn create our entire belief in ourselves and the world surrounding us.

So, when we stop believing we are a separate entity reliant purely on our brain cells to know what direction our boat, our lives, should be going in, it becomes a relief. And when we let in a consciousness that continuously expands and is infinitely creative, we become more than we could ever imagine we are.

When we are able to really feel the presence of our own Light, through learning to allow this to flow through our hearts, we can learn to fine-tune this energy so that the feeling through the heart starts to transfer into conscious thought.

It's more like an inner knowing, an inner Wisdom, that happens in a moment and then becomes a knowing through words. It is experienced very differently to the experience of sitting down to consider something, which creates thoughts in the brain.

Humility helps us to understand that we don't have to know what this is in advance; we simply learn to allow a deep inner listening to occur, which some call meditation and can become way too complicated. In my experience, it's simply listening, not to the physical sounds around you, experienced through the ears, but to the deep inner Wisdom found in the silence of your heart.

My suggestion would be to create a regular, sustained practice of this, beginning perhaps with visualising yourself kneeling in a meadow of flowers and simply seeing what comes.

Donna Collins

Visualisation: Meadow

For this meditation you may choose to kneel instead of sit; however, either way will suffice. In either of these positions find a comfortable posture that allows you to be still in your sacred meditation space. I would also suggest resting your hands comfortably with your palms facing upwards.

Focus on your breath, breathing down into your stomach. Bowing your head slightly, imagine that you are sitting or kneeling in a meadow filled with long grass and tall flowers. As you bow your head, notice that you are the same height as all the flowers.

Notice how that feels in your body; if you feel resistance to this, just notice this, and breathe it out of your body.

Begin to become aware of the sun shining down on you, as it is shining on all the other flowers.

Allow yourself to surrender. There is no comparing yourself to flowers. Allow yourself to simply be with the joy that you are all in the Light of the sun.

Take your attention to your heart and imagine breathing this Light into your heart. Within this Light is Love; feel that Love filling your being.

Gently relax. Keep relaxing and with every breath allow more Light in. It is natural to resist. Simply focus on allowing.

When you are ready, take a couple of deeper breaths, coming back to your body. Open your eyes, returning your awareness to the room that you are in.

With practice, when Love and Light is felt through the heart, it is possible to then allow a question to emerge: 'What is my soul purpose?' I would encourage you to practise the above meditation and next time also ask this question when you feel the Light and Love in your heart. I have included this visualisation again including asking this question for you to practise.

Visualisation: Soul Purpose

Again, for this meditation you may choose to kneel instead of sit; however, either way will suffice. In either of these positions find a comfortable posture that allows you to be still in your sacred meditation space. I would also suggest resting your hands comfortably with your palms facing upwards.

Focus on your breath, breathing down into your stomach. Bowing your head slightly, imagine that you are sitting or kneeling in a meadow filled with long grass and tall flowers. As you bow your head, notice that you are the same height as all the other flowers.

Notice how that feels in your body. If you feel resistance to this, just notice this, and breathe it out of your body.

Begin to become aware of the sun shining down on you, as it is shining on all the other flowers.

Allow yourself to surrender; there is no comparing yourself to other flowers. Allow yourself to simply be with the joy that you are all in the Light of the sun.

Take your attention to your heart and imagine breathing this Light into your heart. Within this Light is Love; feel that Love filling your being.

Gently relax. Keep relaxing and with every breath allow more Light in. It is natural to resist. Simply focus on allowing.

Notice where the tension in your body is that is holding on to your resistance and breathe in and out of this place.

When you feel you can surrender no more, focus your attention on your heart and ask 'What is my Soul purpose?'

Listen to the stillness in your heart and allow yourself to receive the answer. This is not a thought process but a feeling which may bring an image or words within.

If you have received an answer that is more about the everyday, take your attention again to your heart and ask to be shown the bigger picture. 'What is my Soul purpose?'

When you have received an answer or when you feel you are ready, take a couple of deeper breaths, coming back to your body. Open your eyes, returning your awareness to the room that you are in.

For many, this visualisation initially brings a sense of what they need to do in their everyday experience which can include everyday tasks. I encourage you to be grateful for this knowing and then, as I would often suggest to members of a spiritual group I used to facilitate, go back in. This means go back into the felt sense within the heart and ask, 'What else?' Ask your own inner Wisdom to become aware of the bigger picture.

Many people in this moment feel energy in their heart and are surprised by the answer they receive.

This Wisdom can then be used as a compass in your life. Every time you think of doing something you can ask yourself: 'is this in alignment with my soul purpose?' This includes all of those spinning plates!

A note about fulfilling your soul purpose and your destiny

In my experience, certainly writing this book, as I became closer to fulfilling my soul purpose and my destiny, I was met with increased challenges in my life. I felt my life had begun to feel more arduous. I stopped feeling like I was flowing downstream towards my purpose and I wondered at times if I was on the right track.

Although the challenges in my life brought intense feelings of fear and sadness, it felt somehow different to my previous experience of 'the dark night of the soul' described earlier.

I felt as if physical obstacles were placed on my path that had to be overcome in order for me to grow and be ready to reach my destiny of publishing this book and then continue on my spiritual journey.

During this time, a friend shared her joy at spending some time in a local bookshop, just taking in the wonderful expansive and peaceful energy that such places can bring, and I recalled how I also enjoyed this experience very much.

The following day I decided to go to a book shop myself and as usual, I found myself drawn to the spiritual books section. I was immediately drawn to *The Alchemist* by Paolo Coelho, which is a wonderful book about fulfilling your dreams. I bought the book only to find that I had bought it several years ago and already had it at home!

I felt that there must be something very important in the book and when I read it, I believe I received a very important message.

What resonated with me mostly was to read that 'before a dream is realised, all that we have learnt along the way is tested so that in addition to realising the dream, we can master lessons we have learnt as we have moved towards the dream.'

I also learnt the phrase, 'the darkest hour of the night comes before the dawn', which I understood to symbolically reiterate the same meaning, that as one gets closer to fulfilling their destiny, there is often a final or more intense test or challenge.

I experienced this challenge more and more intensely as my writing was nearing the end. What helped me was to recognise that in order to publish my book, I again had to implement all I had learned along the way.

I started to see that in order to fully experience our Light, we have to experience more of our shadow, ultimately experiencing a broader range of emotions, increasing our ability to hold and contain frequencies at both ends of the spectrum of the Rainbow. As we expand one end, the other expands too.

Donna Collins

We can understand this in terms of the psychiatrist Carl Jung's concept of the 'Tree Of Life', which ultimately means that the tree grows up to the Light to the same extent as the roots reach down into the earth.

Therefore, in order to grow or experience Light from our leaves, we have to be prepared for our roots to grow down further into the earth or the dark.

This is another analogy for experiencing our own shadow, our own unconscious, and is part of the work on the spiritual path to the Light. Shortly before I finished writing this book I saw myself in a vision learning to carry a lantern in the darkness in order to find more Light within.

I also started to hear the term 'spiritual warrior' more and more often, and this term was explained to me more fully by a wonderful spiritual guide here in the physical, who shared that a true healer is one who can walk in both the Light and the darkness in order to help others, and it is this ability that is seen as being a warrior.

I realised that the lantern in my vision was also a symbol for myself and for those on the spiritual path; it is essential to understand that in order to experience more Light, we also have to transform our fear of the darkness and look into it in order to bring it into Light.

Sometimes this darkness feels like it is placed over us and in order to find our way out, we are first humbled into surrendering to our Light. This can be a very painful process and for anyone experiencing this I would like to give reassurance that it does pass!

We can also consciously choose to practise humility as part of the journey towards becoming our Light in its fullest and I encourage the following Rainbow Practices:

Rainbow Practices

1. Practise the Meadow visualisation

2. Practise the Soul Purpose visualisation

3. Remember that experiencing difficult and intense feelings is also part of the spiritual journey

Chapter Seven

Grace & Harmony

---

*'Amazing Grace, how sweet the sound,
that saved a wretch like me'*

I once heard Grace described as the oil that allows an engine to *purr*. It takes away the harshness of life experience and softens how we interact in life and with others.

Grace is like having a beautifully kept secret and recognising that it is so immensely sacred that it cannot be shared and will always be respected.

I feel it in my heart as exquisitely beautiful. The sacredness of Grace cannot be compared. During the times I have felt Grace, I experienced a sense of receiving a beautiful, rare and precious gift, like a gift of magic and wonderment mixed together to create a sense of ecstasy at sheer existence.

Faith in Everyday Life | Grace & Harmony

The following visualisation is a wonderful practice to begin to experience Grace:

Visualisation: Light of Grace Through the Leaves

Start again by sitting comfortably in your sacred meditation space. Breathe gently in and out of your nose. Breathe right down into your stomach. Take your attention within and notice again where this is for you.

Take a moment to scan your body, noticing where in your body you are holding any tension and focus on breathing this out, let it go.

Now imagine that you are walking through a beautiful forest. You follow a path that gently winds between the trees.

As you walk you start to feel that you know this place. You have been here before. This knowing feels very nurturing.

You arrive at a circular clearing in the forest and sense that you are somehow being called to pause. You wait. You sense you are here to receive something and excitement fills your body. It feels very special somehow, something important.

In this moment the sun comes out from behind a cloud and you look up at the leaves of the trees above you, which suddenly appear luminous. The Light shining through the leaves is so bright and you know in your being that this is what you are waiting for. Imagine that Grace is the Light shining through the leaves. Feel the Beauty of the Light.

Breathe the Light in and give thanks for the gift of Grace. This Light is for you; smile as you experience Grace.

Take a moment to enjoy being in this space. Take a couple of deeper breaths and gently bring your awareness back to the room that you are in and open your eyes.

If there are Divine feelings, as some religious traditions suggest, then certainly Grace is one of them, alongside Gratitude. What is meant by this is that these feelings are so beautifully subtle and at the 'finer' end of the spectrum of feelings or the Rainbow of Light that they can only be those given by God.

Grace is a form of Beauty, but also brings with it a serenity which is beyond a peaceful experience and more towards the subtle realms of an angelic touch.

Grace also carries, within the gentle breeze that holds it, incredible joy.

Grace is the recognition that in every moment God moves through you, surrounding you and filling you with Love. It is possible to learn to consciously breathe that Love in and feel joy and unconditional Love in every moment. With the experience of Grace comes the experience of upliftment, and this is the magic that happens when we forget our ego false beliefs and are fully present.

Some spiritual traditions suggest that we literally blink in and out of this reality, from spirit to physical form. In every blink, in every breath, there is an opportunity to experience Grace.

How often have you allowed yourself, as per the wonderful words of the great poet William Henry Davies, sufficient 'time to stand and stare'? Poetry often depicts Beauty and Grace, and whether we read this poetry or not, it is something we all have the capacity to feel, if we want to choose a different life, one in which we experience Grace and Faith in the everyday.

In every blinking moment we all can choose to experience Grace and Faith. Or we can choose to run away from the sense of something missing by going back to a distraction. We have all done it – we think about what we have got to *do* instead. We shop or drink or eat or do anything to keep ourselves away from this experience. Or, we can choose to experience the full Beauty and Grace of being an amazing,

Donna Collins

conscious being on a planet which is also alive and breathing, and we can choose to breathe with it.

Imagine that every time you take a breath, you are literally breathing in and out the entire multiverse. The multiverse is constantly expanding and so are you, if you allow yourself.

The reason that Grace and Faith go together is that, just as the light through the leaves on the trees is not always visible, so our awareness of Grace is not always present. Faith is the continuous trust and belief that whether we can still see the Light or not, it is always there.

Prayer is a very powerful way of sustaining awareness of Light and Grace. It is a way of communicating with the Light, and the sheer fact that you are communicating with something you can't see nurtures a stronger awareness of this in the Self. Remember that thoughts are energy. Neuroscientists have found that thoughts create light, a physical light. Scientists are finally confirming what spiritualists have known for hundreds of years! Our thoughts literally create the world in which we live, so when we pray, we set intention for what we choose to experience.

Prayer is a way of asking the Light for something, asking to be shown your path. Many people say to me, 'I pray all the time and never get any answer!'

My question to them is always, 'Do you remember to listen for the response?'

Listening for the answer to prayer is a different practice than listening with our physical ears; it means listening with the heart. It is a very subtle, energetic attunement. It also requires attuning to Grace. This is what is known as meditation.

Listening with the heart is also achieved by the previous practice of humbleness and surrendering. This is so important in learning to attune to Grace. Without the surrendering of the ego and its desire to make something happen, it is very difficult to allow Grace to be felt. So humbleness and Grace also flow together in unison.

The heart does not communicate through words! It is sometimes accompanied by conscious realisations; however, the heart communicates through a feeling, being drawn to someone or something. It's more of an inner knowing and it takes practice to learn to listen in this way.

Donna Collins

Visualisation: Feathers

This is a wonderful visualisation to practise attuning to Grace.

Start by sitting in a chair, or on a cushion on the floor, closing your eyes and taking your attention within, again noticing where within is for you. Everyone is different. Focus on your breath, breathing right down into your stomach. Take your attention to your body and visualise doing a gentle scan of your body, noticing where in your body you are holding any tension and focus on breathing this out.

Turning the palms of your hands upwards, focus on imagining you have a feather resting in each of your hands. Notice the delicate nature of the feather; you know it's there but can hardly feel it and yet you are aware of its strength as it has the capacity to give flight.

Really feel the miracle of the existence of the feather.

Now imagine that you are being completely surrounded and held by feathers. It is overwhelmingly nurturing and holding in a gentle and loving way. You know that this gentleness is also strong enough to hold your entire being and you can completely let go.

Allow yourself to smile a huge smile of relief, in the knowing that you are loved for all that you are. Breathe in and out and enjoy that subtle change within that knows you don't have to do anything, that you are loved unconditionally.

Enjoy being in this moment and when you are ready, take a couple of deeper breaths, bring your awareness back to your body, opening your eyes, back into this physical reality.

How is it to imagine that you are within the feathers the whole time? It's just your awareness that shifts.

This awareness gives us a glimpse that we are 'in the paste' that holds an entire painting together, and the space around us is an illusion.

You are within the Grace of God's Love, always.

It is the illusion of separateness, created by the psyche, that causes so much despair, unhappiness and a feeling of isolation. Doing this practice will over time inevitably bring a smile to your face. Everything you need is right here, always.

When we think of the phrase 'She moves with ease and Grace', what we are really observing is someone who has learnt to surrender their ego desire to the sound of their heart – someone who has learnt humbleness and someone who has complete Trust and Faith in the existence of a greater self, connected with all things in the multiverse. Being in the flow of this brings a sense of floating downstream, an ease that comes without forcing something to happen or continuously trying.

How is it to imagine that it is possible to have a life like this? This does not mean that life does not bring challenges; it does not mean that everything is easy. It doesn't mean that fears do not occur. It means that we have learnt a new way of functioning; we have learnt to listen to all that we are and we are able to use our Faith and Trust as our compass in life so that we have a felt sense of certainty. We are no longer left wondering *what am I here for? What shall I do next?* Our life force, our Light, our creativity is constantly telling us, whispering to us through our heart.

This Wisdom brings a knowing that is unwavering. We know what we are here for. We have a sense of purpose, a soul purpose – the entire reason we are here on this planet, and it really is that profound.

We have spent too long as a human race limiting ourselves to a collection of thoughts in our heads. We have spent literally thousands of years dancing around possibilities and not doing them. After decades of disconnecting with ourselves, we have also disconnected from our home – the planet we live on. We have focused on destruction and limiting ourselves both internally and externally.

Let's consider for a moment the likelihood of you going out tomorrow, getting yourself a pneumatic drill and making a start right in the middle of your living room! Would you do it?! I don't think I need to wait for the answer. It would make absolutely no sense whatsoever for you to start drilling holes in your home. Or would it?

Your planet, the very earth you are on right now, either sitting or standing is your home. And yet, as you read this, someone, somewhere is doing just that. It's called fracking and deforestation and many, many other things and there is a bizarre idea that if it's not in the room you're in right now, that's OK.

Once we fully connect – and by that I mean become fully aware of all that we are – we will stop restricting and hurting ourselves externally, literally just stop. And we can. It can be that simple. Just as if I were to choose right now to stop typing.

We can stop hurting ourselves and this planet. Our outer behaviour is simply a reflection of how we are restricting and hurting ourselves inwardly.

When we learn to cherish and respect ourselves in all our Beauty and learn to honour ourselves, including everything we feel, down to the sheer majesty of the spirit that we are, I have Faith and Trust that our outer world will become a mirror of our inner world. We will naturally have peaceful respect for our home, which is felt in our hearts and includes the amazingly beautiful planet we live on.

This will lead us ultimately to the existence of harmony, being at one with ourselves and the very substance of who and what we are, the very reflection of which is seen by us every day in nature, in the sky and the light and the warmth of the sun.

Harmony: being at one

Writing this chapter, I recalled a wonderful vision in which I was shown everything in the universe and on this planet being in Harmony. I was shown the full extent of what harmony really means.

The vision was extremely vivid. I saw myself sitting in the most beautiful garden. The garden was unlike anything I had ever experienced in the physical. Visions are not just a picture in the mind. Visions are a symbolic image reflecting energetic knowing or communication and so the feeling of the vision is just as important as the image itself.

Therefore although the sense in the vision was of a garden, I was aware, through the feeling, that this was not an individual place, not a separated, enclosed place as we would imagine gardens and parks on earth, in particular in England.

This was a symbolic garden, a vast, endless space with no restriction and no separation. The light and colour in the garden were not something I had seen before with my own physical eyes.

The closest I have seen to this vision was a relatively new type of photography that uses high intensity ultraviolet lights to bring out the glowing florescence in plants. Literally the Light within!

The exquisite beauty of the colour of all the plants and grass in the garden was overwhelming. I experienced the insects and the birds all in their glorious colours too. As well as the colour, I was aware that everything was vibrating, at different frequencies but somehow in harmony. I was struck that the *togetherness* of everything seemed to be conveyed through the sound of the birds and insects and the wind blowing through the grass and the trees.

The full perfection of the vision brought tears to my eyes and I stayed for many moments enjoying the overwhelming feeling of Love that consumed me throughout until I became tired and a sense filled my body that I had received everything I needed to know and I opened my eyes and returned to this physical world.

The vision showed me that Harmony can be understood and felt by considering music, the notes of each instrument

Donna Collins

finely in tune with and complementing all the other instruments so that it is heard as one piece of music.

This is what is happening in our conscious existence, if we choose. Imagine again that everything that we are and everything around us is energy – it is vibration and frequency. In the garden in my vision, I was shown this as a broader spectrum of light than is visible to the human eye or detectable with any man-made machine, at many different frequencies. The garden, a symbol for our entire multiverse, of which we are a part, is sustained and fulfilled through the beautiful Harmony of all the vibrations creating it.

And so harmony is created when we recognise and follow our own natural, innate frequency, which, when integrated with all the other natural, flowing, innate frequencies, creates a state of 'oneness' with all things – a beautiful musical piece of perfection!

What stops us from being in harmony and out of tune is our fear and our thoughts and ultimately not being fully present in the moment as this is when we step away from the present moment, the Wisdom of our hearts and the flowing harmony of the multiverse.

We also separate ourselves from the deeper, more profound aspects of existing as part of the tapestry of a greater picture. We limit our awareness of ourselves and all things to a small, isolated, separate self. In doing so we miss out on the most astonishing experiences that connection brings.

The hugely significant importance of this was experienced by me when I became aware that bird-song is representative of the harmonious nature of the multiverse. It is literally the sound of the universe in harmony. When was the last time you listened to the birds? Do you even notice them? Have you thought that you may be listening to the frequency of God? When you can receive and feel bird-song in your heart, you know you are now finely tuned!

Listen to the Birds practice

Start by positioning yourself either in your meditation space with the window open if you are able to hear birdsong from there or for this practice, you may prefer to find a peaceful place out in nature where you can be fairly sure you will have some quiet in which to listen.

Sit comfortably, with legs crossed on the floor or alternatively on a bench or anywhere comfortable where you can take your attention within.

Close your eyes and begin to take your awareness within, again noticing where this is for you. Focus on your breath, breathing down into your stomach. Do a scan of your body, as you continue to breathe with your eyes closed. Notice where you are holding any tension in your body and focus on breathing this tension out. To release tension breathe in through your nose and breathe out through your mouth as you release.

Notice your body relax, and as you continue to breathe, take your attention to your heart space – first, your physical heart and then to a place that feels like it is behind the heart and gently breathe in and out of this space. Notice your chest expand as you breathe further and further into an infinite expansiveness.

As you sit quietly in the stillness, start to take your attention to the sounds around you. Practise feeling through your heart space the subtle vibrations of the sounds. Then focus your attention on any birdsong you become aware of.

Initially, you will naturally hear this with your physical ears; then again try to focus on the vibration of the sound in the heart space. Don't try too hard; simply repeat sensing the sound through the heart. Imagine that you are a beautiful singing bowl and each sound vibrates through you, causing a resonance with the frequency of each bird.

Practise feeling into this and at the same time become aware of the presence and awareness of the birds. Imagine they also sense your presence!

This practice takes time to heighten your felt sense of the vibration of different frequencies; however, in my experience, it is possible! Ultimately, this practice helps you to open your heart to feel things in a deeper and more subtle way and by doing this it eventually shows us how closed our hearts have been, which is the cause of many feelings of isolation and loneliness for many people.

Harmony begins, as with any relationship, when we begin to realise that we are not 'above' our surroundings, including the people we interact with. It is the realisation that what we are looking at, interacting with, talking with, loving, is at a fundamental level, our very own being.

This state of awareness is possible to glimpse and experience. It relies on the practice of everything stated before in this book; it requires tenacity through allowing Trust within and attention to Beauty.

Experiencing Harmony is the gateway to Grace. Harmony sits, like a new born child, with innocence, held with Love in the lap of Grace.

When Grace is experienced, as the hymn says, 'Grace will lead me home.' Grace ultimately leads to the profound experience of the full majesty of God or consciousness. This comes when we experience being in 'the paste' that holds the whole painting together. When this happens, it would be unthinkable to suggest hurting something around you, as you are, at an energetic level, hurting yourself.

The power of this level of awareness is to truly experience the profound expansiveness and creativeness of what we are consciously breathing in, something bigger than ourselves, and it is then impossible to ever feel alone. Rather than ego-based attempts to feel powerful in order to cover up fear, feeling the majestic power of God through the heart gives us the courage to continue to be ourselves, day after day, without self-doubt creeping in before we go to sleep at night.

Visualisation: Breathing in the Multiverse

Start by focusing on your body, breathing out tension, expanding awareness to the room that you're in. Then expand your awareness to the house that you're in. Gently breathing in and out as you maintain your awareness of your wider surroundings. Now take your attention outward, above the houses, to the road you're in, the town you live in, outwards to include the country that you're in, all the land and the sea, the planet earth and expanding further to space, the planets, the galaxies, the multiverse. Breathe the multiverse in and out.

You may feel a sense of expansiveness in your body, through your heart. Take a moment to feel what this is like. Feel the magnitude and enormity of what you can become conscious of in any moment.

Enjoy this sense of expanse for a few more moments, then gently bring your awareness in, back through space and the galaxies, back to planet earth, down to your own country, your own town, your home, the room that you're in, and now back to your own body. Take a couple of deeper breaths and gently, in your own time, open your eyes.

Grace is, in essence, the awareness of and felt experience of being in harmony with all things in the multiverse. It is being both in the innate flow of your natural vibrational frequency and that of everything around you. When this state is found, life really does begin to feel that you are flowing 'gracefully' downstream.

The subtlety of Grace, when felt through the body, is like the gentle act of altering direction when the wind blows through the sails of a sailing boat; it is not about 'trying' or 'forcing' or 'getting there'. It is the subtle act of feeling, sensing the wind and 'going with.' It requires tiny movements which feel into the direction of the wind, rather than large, less subtle actions. It is a receptive, gentle moving with, rather than something that is acted upon.

Rainbow Practices

1. Practise the Light of Grace through the Leaves visualisation and allow yourself to smile. Write and draw your experiences

2. Pray each day and listen for the answer

3. Practise the Feathers visualisation. Journal Your Experience

4. Listen to the sound and presence of the birds. Feel the harmonic resonance through your heart

5. Practise Breathing In the Multiverse

Chapter Eight

Trust & Truth

Truth is another word for Spirit

Many people find themselves looking for the truth in situations or in life generally or both. When this happens, there is a distinct focus on all things deemed *outer* or *different* to *me*.

I have experienced this when I have observed clients becoming caught up in thoughts about another person or concepts outside of themselves. This prompts repetitive thought processes and questioning such as *What do they mean by that? What are they planning to do? What is their real intention? What is this system we are in? What is life about?*

What they often don't realise is that somewhere within them, albeit unconsciously, they are looking for the fullness of Truth inside themselves. However, by focusing outside themselves, they do the opposite; they come away from themselves and become afraid because ultimately it's another distraction which brings uncertainty as it's almost impossible to know exactly what another person or organisation is intending.

The only certainty is to Trust in what we are intending and what is our Truth.

Truth as another word for spirit, is a sense of trust in the existence of our own Light within us and in everything we experience. This means that in order to experience it, we have to Trust that it is there. This brings the experience of Faith in everyday life.

The practices in this book and the sharing of different concepts will make *no change* to your life if you don't trust and believe it. Remember, all you have to do to experience a complete transformation in yourself and how you experience life is to be open to the concept that you may have forgotten all of who you are. This means being able to Trust. Through trust comes experience and through experience comes Wisdom. In that order.

In many classes I have taken which focus on facilitating others experiencing all that they are, including sensing energy at many different frequencies, the response at the beginning is always, 'I'm not sure if I'm seeing or feeling this or if I'm just making it up.'

In my experience, every time an individual allows themselves to be drawn to experience more of themselves, they start by blocking it with doubt. I have heard many times things like:

> 'I think it might just be my imagination.'

Or

> 'This probably sounds weird...'

Or

> 'I'm probably just making it up.'

Trust is therefore a hugely significant factor in changing awareness of yourself and your experience of life. Trust and belief eventually become Wisdom and Faith.

Trust is also a crucial factor in enabling something that almost every human being finds difficult and that is being with the 'unknown'. The psyche continuously wants to know, even if what it knows is something not good. How many times have you heard someone or yourself say 'I just want to know'?

Donna Collins

That's because if we know, we can busy ourselves by doing something to try to stop the feeling about it.

I imagine this is also part of why the internet Google search is so very popular!

This book gives guidance on being with feelings. Once we can do this, we can be more in the moment. Once we can do this, we can go beyond feelings to experience more of what we really are and this requires Trust.

When we think about Harmony, everything vibrating at a frequency that flows with everything else, we can imagine that if we try to force something to happen, through fear of it not happening, we automatically shift and change our frequency, and we find ourselves in situations that don't feel right and don't go well - we become out of tune.

Trust is also part of allowing. If we go back to the visualisation of breathing with the universe, we start to experience that it is constantly expanding and also, rather than contracting, we can start to imagine that what is actually happening is that it is also flowing to us. We expand out with the universe and it then flows to us at the natural frequency that we are, if we allow it.

My own experience of this brought huge realisations for me. It was hugely profound to sense through my body, breathing in through my nose and lungs, the possibilities and Wisdom of the multiverse.

I remember being at home, sitting in the quiet on the sofa, as I often did. I focused on my breath and a sense of peace filled my body. A vision of the cosmos filled my mind with its infinite expanse. Through the image came a feeling of the beauty of the physical aspects I could see, the light of the stars and galaxies and the vastness of space, which I initially saw as black *nothingness*.

This was followed by a wave of excitement that started in my heart and flowed through my body. I sensed something else in the blackness. New wisdom flowed through me that this was not *nothing*. This was *everything*, infinite Wisdom and intelligence that had a capacity to respond to my frequency with the same frequency.

I realised it wasn't just still; beyond the blackness was a flowing energy, like the under current in a river that moves when the surface appears still. This flowing energy moved towards me when I breathed in. It resonated with what I was feeling.

As I became more excited, more energy flowed and when I then became joyous about my new-found Wisdom, a new frequency of *joy* flowed towards me too.

Donna Collins

It sounds impossible to those still intellectualising. In my experience, it is not.

This new wisdom changed my life because I realised that if I focused on my frequency, energy would naturally flow back to me and that meant that this energy brought with it physical manifestations, people and experiences that allowed me to continue to feel the same. I realised that the alternative concept of working hard to *get things* and *succeed* was not the Truth.

All I had to do was focus on my inner energetic frequency or state.

The Beauty of this was that as I let go of trying, I became more in the flow of my own frequency and things happened in my life. Clients were referred to me, work just flowed and a new relationship began. And I continued to feel the Light that I am.

This book asks you to trust that it is possible – if you believe, if you can imagine. Some believe imagination is evidence of the Divine. They cannot be separated and you are reading this book for a reason! You are reading this book because somewhere within you, you have been drawn to do so and you have either picked the book up at this page or you have been drawn to keep reading!

Trust comes when you start to recognise that place within you that calls. That place that is intrigued and curious. I wonder if you can pause for a moment right now…? Where do you feel that curiosity in your body? Keep your attention there for a moment; breathe in and out of that place, get to know it. Learn to trust it and you are learning to trust the very thing I am writing about!

It is also essential to trust when things happen that you think you don't want. As the Dalai Lama said, 'Sometimes not getting what you want is a wonderful stroke of luck!' Can you trust that there is a greater knowing both within and around you that already knows your true frequency better than you do and is helping you create a life that allows you to live it?

All you need to do is learn to get out of the thoughts in your head that talk you out of it!

This book asks you to Trust that deep within you, you already know what you need. This book also asks you to Trust that by reading this book you are learning to remember!

This whole book until now is giving you tools to use to access your Light, the Light that is connected with all things and is flowing towards you and through you at all times.

Donna Collins

This is the Light that also knows your purpose, as stated in Chapter 6, the very reason you are on this planet.

Trust is the key to you living your purpose, every day. For this to happen, you first need to become aware of your purpose and then allow yourself to be drawn, by trusting, to find a way to live in alignment with it. If you have not realised your purpose, it is almost inevitable that, as well as your psyche restricting you, your external circumstances are also out of alignment with your own Light. By that I mean that your external environment is not at the same frequency – out of tune – with your instrument, or in reality, your instrument is out of tune with your environment.

This tells me that right now, for you, life is hard. I imagine it often feels like you are trudging uphill. You will frequently feel like something is missing, you will experience loneliness and you may also question, 'What *is* the point?'

The point is, the thing that is missing is your awareness and fulfilment of your own Light.

I imagine you are also living a perceived reality in which you tell yourself things like:

> 'I have to work hard to enjoy life.'

Or

'Work is a means to an end.'

You also accept relationships in your life that are unfulfilling, that leave you feeling drained and often sad.

These circumstances can also give you the insight that simply says you are out of Harmony, with yourself and your surroundings, including people. And some of those people will be those you love; however, you may still experience no upliftment, because you are vibrating away from your true frequency in order to be with them and for them to feel better.

Trust brings with it a further need for surrender. It can be really difficult initially to accept that Trusting and following your own purpose and path in life means that your external world may change and that includes the people in it.

In my experience, during my own awakening, it was literally like an instant revelation to recognise that life was not at all as I had imagined it to be. At 39 years old, I stood and looked in the mirror, after my dad had passed away, and asked, 'Why has no one told me about this?!'

I felt like I had stepped outside myself. I was experiencing the immense beauty of the energetic consistency and harmony of reality, which included me, and then looking at myself in my physical body and seeing how closed off I was, neither able to see nor perceive this Beauty.

Donna Collins

I was so focused on the small identity I had created. I was Donna, the youngest child who now worked in finance, a separate human being, a physical body with an ego will and desire and a belief in that smallness, and I was completely blind to anything greater than that.

I experienced some anger initially. How could I have reached the end of my 30s, busy trudging up my own hill, believing that's what I 'should' be doing in life in order to make ends meet, in a corporate environment that felt dull and arduous?

I then felt panic, my ego was responding with fear of destruction in some way. I felt overwhelmed, as if just landing on a new planet. Nothing was as I thought it was. I was not separate at all; there was literally a world, an energetic multiverse of light and colour, that I had no idea was there before.

As I stayed with the fear, and breathed, it gradually subsided. In the moment that followed, it became clear to me that I was remembering and seeing myself, my Light, my own being and it took a catalyst of bereavement to help me to do this.

The experience was literally like being plugged in. All my senses were heightened, the vibrant colour of life outside was incredible, like I had never seen the sky before, and I knew in some ways I had been asleep and I had just woken up.

I was seeing the true vibration of the world, our beautiful planet, and I knew that this beautiful light of many many colours, that also flowed through me, was not being allowed to express itself fully.

I had to change my life completely and after this moment of realisation, I did exactly that. Everything in my life changed. My career, my home, my relationship.

My awareness had changed. I could now feel everything in my life, apart from the love of my family and friends, was out of Harmony with the Beauty I had felt and continued to experience.

This was not easy. I was identified with these things and I was afraid. It took time but I found that new opportunities came to me. I was offered redundancy, and the draw to train at a specific place in London was so in alignment with Beauty that I could not do anything else and so it was logistically impossible to continue to live where I was.

My relationship was something I had known was not right for a long time. I recognised that fear of being alone had kept me in it, which I observe is the case for many clients in therapy initially.

My new sense of all that is – the sheer Beauty of the Love and Light that we are, that had flowed through me, unhindered, in those previous moments – eventually became much stronger than the fear of staying. The relationship ended and I moved away.

We can think about what we create in our lives like a spider in a web. We set about, mostly unconsciously in life, creating things we think we 'should' do in order to be accepted. We are the spider, we create a web, somewhere we think we should be, and we spend hours, days, months, years creating it. We even believe on a certain level that we like it! It's a well-created web, and we often have visitors over who get stuck in it too!

So, when we step back and look at the spider, do we see a spider which has created a beautiful web of Light that it can choose to change at any time? Or do we see a spider that is stuck in an everlasting web of trudge?

The reason we often feel stuck is that the things we create are our attachments, the things that simply stop us feeling afraid. They are not always the things we truly love nor do they allow us to be all that we are. The 'stuck' feeling is actually that we don't really want them, but we need them to keep fear at bay.

This book is a way for you to remember to choose to leave your web without fear keeping you in it and without something traumatic happening to you causing you to drop out, although this may be the case for you too.

I encourage you to make the choice, to choose to trust a deeper calling within you. In my experience, this calling happens in subtler ways throughout life anyway but often goes unheard.

Only you know your true thoughts and feelings, like the ones that happen when you lie awake at night or first thing in the morning when you wake up, before your psyche has a chance to cover them up with doing something.

Think about every time you tell yourself you *should* be doing something or you *shouldn't*. Allow yourself to really feel all the things you are doing in your life that you don't really want to. How many of the things in your external world do you do because you love them?

To choose to trust can also bring feelings of sadness. Often people start to grieve the number of years they have done things they didn't really want to do and having a level of sadness over this is understandable.

It is also temporary. Ask yourself *do I want to have this realisation again in ten years? Do I want to feel sad again then?*

Donna Collins

Visualisation: Trusting & Floating Downstream

Sit in your sacred meditation space. Take a few moments to simply breathe and feel at one with your cushion or place in the room.

Close your eyes and take your attention within. Notice again where within is for you today. Focus on your breath, breathing right down into your stomach.

Imagine today that you have decided to change things in your life. It is a bright, sunny day and you leave the house to go to a river that you know of nearby.

When you reach the water's edge there is a paddle boat waiting for you; you feel somehow that this is yours and it would be OK to take, so you get in.

As you sit in the boat, you start to paddle to get moving. As you do this you think about all the things you have done in your life before and all the things that you do now that you really don't want to do – all the people you see that you don't really want to see, the job you feel you 'ought' to do.

As you think of this, the paddle feels heavier and heavier. You can't hold on any more.

In this moment you feel a sense within you that there is something more to you, something that is strong and unbreakable. The very thing you have been using to keep paddling, you now use to stop and let go of the paddling. You choose instead to trust this part of you to simply be in this boat instead and let it take you to where you need to be.

You keep telling yourself to float downstream, all I need to do is stop paddling upstream. I don't even have to turn my boat around! Just stop.

As you stop paddling you feel sad as you feel time has been wasted. Allow yourself to lie back in the boat and let the beauty of the water take you where you need to be.

Allow yourself to feel the sadness, in the knowing that it will pass just as you are continuing to flow in your boat. Then make a choice to trust that somehow this river knows where you need to be, that the strength you had to keep your life the same can be used to create new experiences.

Trust that this is happening to create space for you to create a life you love, being the Light that you are. You notice for the first time the sun shining on the water, and you hear the gentle breeze through the leaves on the trees. You hear the birds singing and you notice that you are smiling in the gentle letting go of all that was.

As you surrender, you move further down the river, away from everything you always thought you should be and you feel relief.

A sudden thought fills your mind. How do I change things now?' You sit up and pick up your paddles, ready to carry the weight again. Instead you Trust that it's OK to feel sad at the moment as you know it will pass.

You put the paddles down again and relax into a comfy cushion that has now appeared in the boat with you. You breathe in the warm air and feel the sun shining down on your skin. You notice for the first time the name painted on the boat is 'Trust'. You tell yourself I've come back for you, I'm not leaving you again.

Take a few moments to enjoy being in this space, floating downstream, sensing that it is OK to not know where you are going right now.

Then take a couple of deeper breaths, bringing your attention back to the room that you are in and when you are ready, open your eyes.

This visualisation can be a very powerful way to learn to Trust yourself and learn to sit with feelings rather than rush by them with thoughts and doing things to distract.

Thoughts of *How?* come when we stop and accept that there is another way. This is your psyche impatiently wanting to know as it is attempting to avoid sadness of how your life has been until now.

And so the visualisation encourages you to choose another way in this moment. Choose not to leave yourself this time; tell yourself, 'I've come back for you… I'm not leaving you again.' Ensure that you do not rush to know *how*. Honour your sadness and by doing this you will not be busy trying to find another distraction to keep you away from this feeling.

And you will find, if you don't rush, if you honour yourself and your feelings about your past, you will feel better. You will feel stronger.

You will pass through forgiveness, forgiving yourself for choices you have made and through understanding and compassion for you, for the fact that you had not, up until now, realised that by 'doing', you had come away from yourself.

By pausing, you are creating space for Trust and Truth to enter into your heart.

By doing this, you are learning to Love, yourself, first and foremost. This is so important for two reasons. Firstly, you then in turn, understand how to love others. Secondly, you start to experience that this Love is fundamentally what you are. This is the true energetic frequency that enables Harmony in life and ultimately, all things in the multiverse.

Donna Collins

You have been trying, potentially all your life, to somehow get this love from others. You have been jumping through hoops to get people to accept you so that they love you. You distract yourself again from your fears of being unlovable and you feel good about yourself. Ultimately, you are the very thing you've been trying to get.

When you have this felt experience through your body, it feels like coming home. There is an immense realisation that there is nothing to be 'done'. You never needed to seek acceptance from others. You were being called to accept yourself and all of who you are.

I remember the first time I experienced this. It was the weekend, several years ago when I had begun training as a psychotherapist. The training was experiential and involved several weekends, which were always a totally immersive experience.

I was driving to London for one of the weekends. It was the summer and as I drove, I noticed the blue sky, and the weather was warm, which felt very nurturing. I joined the motorway and drove for some time. I thought about the training to come and experienced some excitement and anticipation about the learning and growth that had always occurred on these weekends over the years I had trained so far.

As I drove nearer to London a flock of green parakeets flew across the motorway. I was in awe. I wasn't aware that parakeets had been released in London several years before and to see them fly low down, in front of my car, created a real sense of wonderment within me. It felt very surreal to see a flock of tropical birds over a London motorway!

I smiled and in that moment experienced a huge wave of gratitude and joy through my body. I smiled again at the acknowledgement of the beauty of the earth and all its wonderful creatures.

As I continued to drive, a continued feeling of warmth filled my being. I noticed the feeling was very familiar, I recognised it as Love. I said out loud, 'This is who I am', and continued to smile.

I had been single for a number of years and when I felt this Love I realised for the first time in my life that I was not receiving this from someone. It was not because I was *in love* with someone else. It was there within me the whole time, it was me.

I knew in that moment my searching was done. I never needed to look for Love from someone else again. I was home. I no longer needed someone else to prove I was loveable. If I was ever in a relationship again, it would be for other reasons, to share and enhance my life.

Donna Collins

The Love that you are is what has drawn you to read this book…

What comes with this realisation and acceptance and the sense that there is 'nothing to be done' is a prevailing peace and calmness in your life.

Can you now commit yourself to this way of being? Can you continuously remind yourself of your Truth? And live by it?

Do you trust and believe that it is possible to live each day like this? Effectively having, experiencing, living, breathing Faith in every day? When the fullness of Trust enters your heart and way of being, a new strength is experienced, deep inner clarity that brings knowing and certainty. This is far, far away from the busy, distracted self that is simply covering up fear.

The new inner strength that flows into the heart is unbreakable; it has therefore no wall of defence and so there is no need to try to cover up. It simply is.

When this happens, you will experience the world and life differently. You will start to recognise that everything in existence is energy, all at different frequencies, and you will start to function differently, if you Trust.

Visualisation: White Horse

This visualisation provides space for you to practise Trust.

Start by finding a comfortable chair or cushion to sit on. Ensure your feet are on the ground if on a chair and your back is supported.

Close your eyes and take your attention within. Notice where in your body within is for you. Then breath gently down into your stomach. Breath out all the tension in your body.

Imagine that you are standing outside on a path that leads through a forest on a dark, winter, moonlit night. You are wrapped in a warm coat and you see your breath appear as it meets the cold air. The moon illuminates the path and you feel safe.

You look ahead with expectation and see a magnificent white horse walking towards you. It stops near you and you are in awe at its incredible beauty. You realise you know this horse well.

You become aware that only the horse knows the way through the forest. It has no saddle as it is completely free. You know you need to Trust this horse to carry you to where you need to be.

You manage to climb onto the horse's back and it feels very comfortable, like an easy reclining chair and you lie back, looking up at the stars, hearing the gentle sound of the horse's breath and you relax and let the horse take you along the path to where you need to be.

Notice what it feels like to Trust in the horse. Notice how you can relax and enjoy the ride when you are not afraid of letting go.

Notice where outside of the forest the horse is carrying you to.

When you feel that you have seen what you need to know, gently climb down off the horse and thank the horse for its guidance.

Then gently take a couple of deeper breaths, opening your eyes and breathing gently back in your surroundings.

This visualisation assists in the practice of Trust. The white horse is a symbol for the Light or the Spirit within. The more you can Trust the horse, the more you will be able to Trust your own Light.

Rainbow Practices

1. Practise the Trusting and Floating Downstream visualisation. Write and draw your experiences

2. Practise the White Horse visualisation

Chapter Nine

Beauty & Magnificence

"All things bright and beautiful"

Beauty is the feeling we experience when we look out at a stunning landscape. For me, standing on a hillside, taking in the view of a hill or mountain in front of me with the contrast of colour against a blue sky is an experience of perfection.

All of my senses heighten to take in the wholeness of the scene – the smell, the breeze on my skin, the warmth of the sun, the sound of nature, the birdsong, the wind gently kissing the leaves on the trees as it flows through them.

Within this experience is a sense of no separateness. It becomes more of an experience of being at one with the scene that was initially in front of me and now consumes my very being.

Donna Collins

Just as the wind appears to gently kiss the leaves, the experience of the beauty of nature can also be one of mutual affection. Imagine that as you smile at nature, it smiles right back at you. This warm affection, if you allow your heart to open, can bring with it a feeling of unconditional love and admiration.

Visualisation: Smiling at Beauty

Start again by sitting comfortably in your own sacred space, ensuring that your back is supported. Close your eyes and take your attention within, again noticing where 'within' is for you today. Breathe down into your stomach. Notice where in your body you are holding tension and focus on breathing this out gently with every breath.

Imagine that you are standing on top of a hillside. It is a sunny day with blue skies and whispy, white clouds. There is a valley down in front of you and you can see the hill on the other side; notice how green and lush it is with the gently sloping and rising contours on the top of the hill. Notice the wonderful contrast in colours of green and blue. Feel the warmth of the sun on your skin and the breeze on your face, the smell of the country and the sound of the birds.

Smile at the scene in front of you. Imagine that nature is smiling back at you. Notice how this feels. Sense that you somehow know this place very well. You are smiling with a knowing, an inner wisdom that somehow you both know each other. Feel the warmth of this knowing and fondness. Feel the love of the final seeing of a forgotten friend.

Now imagine that the scene is somehow moving towards you. Imagine yourself being drawn into the scene – the warmth and freshness at the same time, a feeling of joy and affection in your heart. Imagine that you have become one with the perfection of nature.

Enjoy being in this place for a few more moments and then when you are ready, taking a couple of deeper breaths bring your awareness back to the room that you are in, back to your body and open your eyes when you are ready.

Other people may find beauty when looking at different scenes; however, the same concept still applies. The experience of seeing and feeling the perfection of nature is like looking into a mirror. It reflects the Beauty that is also within us, to which we can also respond with a feeling of affection, warmth and Love.

At the ultimate energetic level, we are nature. We are the very thing that we are looking at. Conceptually, you are smiling at yourself! You are perfect, just as you are!

Donna Collins

The reason we feel the Beauty of the scene so deeply is that we are not judging it. When we see something as perfect, we are not then putting some of our energy into resisting part of it.

Imagine if instead of simply taking in the scene with every aspect of our being, we started using our thoughts to judge. We would go up into our heads, focusing instead on words and tell ourselves *'Well I don't like that tree, that's not bending and growing in the way it should. I like the light and colour there and not here.'*

What happens when we do this is we are no longer present energetically with all of our being. We are only part *there* as the other part is busy using energy to judge instead and our sense of connection, our immersion in the scene, subsides and we create that sense of separateness.

This is what we are doing when we perceive other human beings and ourselves. Ultimately, when we judge, we are not fully present in our lives and we lose our capacity to experience the full immersive state of Beauty.

An example of this shows itself when we consider that through out humanity, Beauty has often been associated with women or the feminine. It is very striking that the human psyche sees Beauty often more in one gender more than another.

I have used this example as thousands of years ago, the Alchemists believed that as spirit, we spiral down through the heavens, initially made up of the four elements of nature – earth, fire, air and water – and when we incarnate we undergo our first separation, that of spirit into matter, or bodily form, and from here, we undergo a further divide into masculine and feminine.

The primary separation from spirit in Transpersonal psychology is thought to be the original wound for all human beings and our yearning to be reunited with spirit is our sense of what many call being *home,* the feeling of complete unconditional love, nurturing and acceptance. It is thought that this yearning for home is our primary unconscious motivation to be in relationships as it reminds us of the unity we experience before we come into a physical body.

We can view the divide into masculine and feminine energies as two opposites and we can also then begin to understand that these opposites create the beginning of all human experience as one of duality.

It is possible to help us heal the original separation from spirit by becoming aware of every opposite in our experience, at every level, everything that we perceive as ourselves and not ourselves. We can also get to know our own masculine and feminine energy.

Donna Collins

In mythology and alchemy, the sun has often represented the masculine, whereas the moon is associated with the feminine. These two energies are experienced very differently, the sun being very fiery and active and also associated with physical 'Light' or Spirit, whilst the moon is calm and receptive and associated with physical 'darkness' or matter. The masculine, in its powerful, active nature, can be deemed as 'positively charged'.

The feminine, lovingly peaceful, receptively receiving, holding energy can also be deemed as 'negatively charged' and can also be felt as a stillness, a nurturing, and within this, a Beauty.

As symbols of these two energies, let us again consider the sun and the moon. Which is more beautiful? Of course, both have Beauty, experienced in different ways. Yet when it comes to the human race, we generally seem to have a natural ability to see and experience Beauty in the feminine whereas it does not occur as naturally to many when we consider the masculine.

This is even more striking when we consider that these two concepts are really not about gender at all. They are simply two different energies manifest in the physical that both come from the Light of Creation. These two energies are within every human being, regardless of gender and are both from the same source of Beauty and Love.

By seeing Beauty in one and not the other, we are resisting and not accepting one fundamental part of ourselves. And here is the very beginning of the work of the psyche, to keep the parts of us we do not accept in the unconscious. From the beginning we limit ourselves, effectively to half of ourselves, symbolically living life with one arm tied behind our backs.

Our perception of what we see as good or bad, beautiful or not, is a fundamental aspect of being a conscious human being. This filters down into everything we see ourselves as and what we ultimately reject, from being a man and not a woman, to being spiritual or not spiritual, being rich not poor, educated or not. At every level we create opposites, inevitably rejecting one of them as 'not me' and at every level we unwittingly take ourselves further away from experiencing the full perfection of Beauty that we are.

In order to truly experience the perfection and power of Beauty, we must learn to integrate all perceived opposites. This includes loving all of ourselves and becoming understanding and accepting of things we deem as 'not us'. We also need to learn to see that there is Beauty in everything around us, not just in the things we like.

To do this, we again need to practise compassion. The meaning of compassion in a dictionary is 'the feeling or emotion, when a person is moved by the suffering or distress of another, and by the desire to relieve it.'

Donna Collins

However, in practice, the embodied experience of compassion is much more than this. We can imagine compassion as a gently flowing, clear water stream, glistening in the light, that flows through our experience of ourselves, others and all things.

Visualisation: Experiencing the Flowing Stream of Compassion

Start again by sitting comfortably in your sacred meditation space, closing your eyes and taking your attention within. Focus on your breath, breathing down into your stomach.

Imagine yourself in your life as an image of nature, with yourself either as you, a human being, or as an animal or a flower. Imagine that there is a stream flowing through your image. Notice how crystal clear the water is and you see how it is intricately flowing through every aspect of the scene you are seeing, touching the grass, the flowers, the animals, being drawn up into the sky to flow back down again as rain.

You become aware of the purity of the water, the gentleness it brings and the warm reassurance of life and love, the gentle flow that brings all aspects of your picture, your image, together.

Now imagine this stream is the quality of Compassion, bringing a gentle flow of softness and loving attention and empathy and understanding to everything it touches.

Spend some time in this place; notice your body relax with the soothing of the gentle waters of compassion and when you are ready, take a couple of deeper breaths, bringing your awareness back to the room that you are in, back to your body and again, gently open your eyes.

Compassion

Often we struggle to understand others. Compassion helps us to empathise, relate to and feel the struggles of another. It is the feeling that ensures that we don't fall into self-righteousness. Compassion enables us to recognise our human propensity to either place ourselves above others as an attempt to avoid our own wounds, or place ourselves below others by idealising them and reaffirming our beliefs that we are not good enough. This means we are then able to see ourselves as equals, recognising our shared humanity.

A compassionate response or state is really the opposite of judging. When we find ourselves judging another, we separate ourselves. We find ourselves thinking inwardly *Oh that's terrible, I would never do that,* or conversely *Of course they have done well or got away with that, It's because life is always easy for them.'*

Donna Collins

Judging takes us away from compassion. A compassionate response would be one of empathy to both the other and ourselves. For example we can stop to feel what it might be like for the other person. We may not have been through exactly the same set of circumstances; however, we can understand what it might feel like for them.

We can understand also that even if one thing in a person's life is going well, they will also have challenges too, as we do ourselves. We can have understanding for ourselves that we are on a different path and understand and feel empathy for our own life experience.

Ultimately, compassion comes from a sense and feeling of our shared experience of what it is to be human, rather than focusing on the difference in the life story at the time.

We can also recognise that our energetic state is reflected in the deepest psychological beliefs that have been part of human existence since it began for example a deep underlying perception that the receptive, holding, peaceful, nurturing energy of the feminine, as well as being beautiful, is somehow weak and, in the vast majority of cases, only applicable to women.

This distorted image of the feminine has filtered through into the perception of what it means to be a woman for centuries, with the inner feminine being rejected for being weak by both genders, and women have identified with this by historically adopting a more subservient role.

Although the two energies of masculine and feminine are formless, we can imagine them by using the image of a lava lamp. For those who do not know what this is, it's a lamp that has flowing liquid within. The liquid has bubbles within it that differ in colour and these bubbles float round the lamp gradually changing shape and size. Imagine the bubbles are orange and the rest of the liquid blue.

As the bubbles change shape and size, the remaining blue has to change shape and size too because the bubbles are retained within the lamp. This can be seen as working in synergy. This also happens to masculine and feminine energy within a human being. If one energy becomes out of balance, or is taking up too much space in the lamp, the other is affected too.

Therefore the distorted image of the feminine inevitably creates a distortion in the image of the masculine too.

This image has led to a belief by men and women that the masculine should be in some way unfeeling and has created a need to control the feminine in physical form as well as our planet, Mother Nature herself. This need to control has also filtered into governments, industries and business.

Donna Collins

Ultimately, what has been manifested is an untrue stereotype and belief of what it is to be a man and a woman. And here we are, as a human race, with a distorted self-image, both masculine and feminine, not really knowing why we have somehow come away from ourselves.

Masculine and feminine, active and receptive, spirit and matter are all opposites manifest from the same creative light and all of these aspects are within you whether you are a man or a woman.

The full Truth of the Beauty of the manifest God has gone unseen by mankind throughout history. And now is a time for change, because YOU are the manifest God, every opposite on every level. When we get to know these opposites and we integrate them, we are able to experience the utmost level of Beauty in the physical.

The experience of integrating every opposite within you is a gift for healing. It is an opportunity to return to your natural, innate frequency of Light and ultimately a life filled with a sense of wholeness.

In order to integrate any opposite it is necessary to know both opposing aspects. Therefore in order to integrate your own masculine and feminine, it is necessary to have an idea of how these energies have manifested within you.

These will be in the form of your qualities as well as aspects of you that create challenges for you in life.

Both your qualities and challenges can be masculine or feminine and it would be easy to include more details here of what is often deemed by psychologists, psychotherapists or energy practitioners to be masculine or feminine, such as one being more active or passive than the other; however, in my experience, what is important here is how each individual experiences this for themselves and what you feel is applicable to you.

To do this, we can again use a guided visualisation for us to access our unconscious and see what our masculine and feminine energies literally look and feel like to you. Alternatively again, you may wish to draw what you imagine after you have read the guided visualisation.

Remember again that there is no *'right or wrong'* in anything you experience either in a visualisation or when you draw. The more you can simply go with what comes to you, the more you will access the true reflection of your unconscious energetic make-up.

Donna Collins

Visualisation: Inner Masculine & Feminine

Start by sitting comfortably, keeping both feet flat on the floor, closing your eyes when you are ready and taking your attention within. Focus on your breath, breathing right down into your stomach.

Now imagine that you are walking along a path in a forest. Take in the Beauty of the nature around you. Now looking ahead, you become aware that your inner masculine is waiting to the right of the path ahead. Notice what he is like, how he looks; take in his qualities and the things you notice that he perhaps finds challenging. Notice how he approaches you and what he has to say to you.

Imagine that you continue walking on with him and ahead on the left side of the path is your inner feminine. Notice what she is like, how she looks; take in her qualities and what you notice she is less comfortable with about herself. Notice how she now approaches your inner masculine, and how they interact with each other.

Then continuing on the path, thanking them for showing themselves and gently when you are ready, opening your eyes and come back into the room.

I encourage you to draw or note down what you have seen and spend some time reflecting on the two characters you have seen in the visualisation or in your drawing.

What stands out to you about the characters? With both the masculine and feminine, see if you can notice how they are, who they are as well as how they look. What qualities do you see in them? What do you notice about aspects of them that are perhaps not so developed? Really get to know them.

This is you! You are seeing yourself in these two characters.

I would also suggest then that to keep these characters fresh in your awareness, you practise in the every-day considering when you react to something, asking yourself the question *Is this my inner masculine or feminine responding?*

Consider whether it is the strengths and qualities of either the masculine or feminine or the more undeveloped aspects within you that are responding.

This is simply as you have seen them, not what you think it should be or how they should be.

Also take time to regularly visualise your inner feminine and masculine conversing with each other. How can they help and support each other? This is helping you to start to integrate these two energies.

This takes time and practice and eventually will help you start to experience more wholeness and the full wonderment of Beauty.

When this occurs, the path towards experiencing the magnificence of God shows itself.

Magnificence

Imagine a beautiful black horse. Notice the incredible Beauty. Within the Beauty lies a magnificence that is so difficult to define in words. The word is more often used to describe something that has immense presence, like a horse or a lion. Magnificence also applies to both masculine and feminine energies.

Magnificence can only be experienced through an appreciation of and a felt sense of Beauty of both of these energies through the body, which in my experience only happens when we heal the opposites within and start to experience wholeness in every facet of our lives.

In other words, the way to sense God's magnificence flowing through you begins with the experience of Beauty, which comes through experiencing wholeness. This can be a hugely profound experience.

I experienced magnificence only after I had started on the path to integrating the opposites within me and I had stopped imagining all things spiritual as being something outside of myself. Whenever I had done this I was placing all magnificence outside of me and what I could feel through a sense of beauty was limited as my energy was still busy working hard at suppressing all the aspects of myself I didn't accept and love.

Then I was humbled. This happened through the trauma of bereavement initially, which created a spiritual experience and intense heart opening. As this happened, my ego, my psyche and all its defences were broken down, and my soul made its presence known. An inner strength and presence that I had never been fully aware of showed itself. It was like a dirty window that was instantly cleaned and the Light shone through in all its Glory.

So what is holding us back from experiencing the magnificence and power we see in something like a horse in everything? Why is it different when we look at a bird? Why is it we either need a traumatic experience or to see things in the physical in order to reflect it back to us?

When we really think about and feel the absolute miracle of being alive and conscious on a planet that is spinning around in nothingness, what stops us from experiencing magnificence in everything?

Donna Collins

Certain things appear to be more striking, perhaps because some experiences are more rare, like if you were to see a kingfisher or a being you had never seen before or travelled to somewhere with a landscape you had never seen before.

The rare experiences are actually glimpses into our true reality; they are literally a wake-up call.

Basically, we, as humans, have become numb to our environment over time. We stop experiencing it fully and in my experience during my awakening of heightened sensory awareness, I can share that this is an illusion. We are surrounded in every moment by the magnificence of creation and we don't see it, we don't feel it because we are numb to it, and we don't attend to it because we are distracted by our busyness of life.

The profound realisation that comes with this knowing is that we are numb to ourselves. We do not see our own true magnificence and that is why we don't experience it all the time, every day when we look around us.

The journey towards experiencing magnificence begins when we start to open to the realisation of who we really are, when we get to know and integrate the opposites within us, and a sense of wholeness presides which allows our Light to flow through our heart.

The Light flows fully when there is no longer rejection of any part of the self and so in order to experience it fully it is essential to heal any opposite that has been rejected.

Beauty is the felt sense of experiencing our full Light within. It is a gentle, holding and receptive energy as well as an active, assertive, creative fire that includes the experience of wonderment, a sense of overwhelming, breathtaking Love, admiration and magnificence in every moment.

Beauty and magnificence can never be forced. Instead it is an experience of opening up to and allowing. In essence, Beauty opens her arms and calmly welcomes you in and magnificence greets you.

Rainbow Practices

1. Practise the Smiling At Beauty visualisation. Write and draw your experiences

2. Practise the Flowing Stream of Compassion visualisation

3. Practise the Inner Masculine and Feminine visualisation. Draw your experiences

Chapter Ten

Gratitude

'How Great Thou Art'

Gratitude is a beautiful feeling of continued wonderment and a certain sense of fulfilment and achievement. It is a sense of having a dream come true. There is no longer any striving to do and an unbelievable felt sense through the body of somehow having made it. With this sense is a relief; it can be felt like having climbed a steep, arduous mountain and finally made it to the top. Now there is nothing more to do other than rest, look around and admire your achievement in a stunningly beautiful resting place, thankful for the strength, tenacity and perseverance you have put into the climb and for being able to keep going when things were really tough.

To help experience the feeling of gratitude we can practise the following:

Visualisation: Mountain Top Gratitude

Sit comfortably in your sacred meditation space. Close your eyes and breathe down into your stomach. Breath out any tension in your body and take a moment to simply focus on your breath.

Imagine yourself at the foot of a huge mountain. You look up and notice that you are unable to see the top as it is so high. You check out the terrain and you can see that although some of the mountain path is clear and edged with green grass, you can see that there are places going up the mountain that seem more difficult; there are rocks to scramble over and there is water to cross.

You recognise this mountain as the symbol of your life. You know that this mountain is your journey and although you have some apprehension, you are also excited about the possibilities and who you may become as you walk your path.

Allow yourself to imagine that you walk and climb for many days, sometimes in good weather, surrounded by blue skies and warm sunshine, and sometimes in pouring rain and wind and yet you manage to keep going.

After many days you reach the top. You made it!

You find a comfortable rock to sit on and take in the exhilarating feeling, a sense of achievement, and at the same time relief fills your being and you are grateful to have been able to continue during all the times when things were difficult, when you were tired and feeling unable to continue – when your feet hurt and you felt lonely and upset.

You start to feel proud of yourself and your achievement. You recognise your own inner strength and determination and your ability to simply keep going despite the challenges you faced. You see your qualities that have enabled you to complete the climb and you smile with admiration for yourself and the mountain in all its grandeur.

As you sit, a sense comes over you that everything you had been striving for, everything you dreamed you would be, you already are.

You sense again relief in your body – a letting go of trying. In the space, a wave of energy flows through your body. Excitement and anticipation again fills your being.

Imagine shouting the words out across the mountain top, 'I've made it!'

Now imagine that you feel overwhelmingly thankful that you have made it… This is the feeling of gratitude.

Stay in the feeling of gratitude. Enjoy being in this place of contentment. Then when you are ready, taking a couple of deeper breaths, open your eyes and come back to the room that you're in.

Gratitude is also a frequency felt within the body, the felt sense of which can be used to both continue and enhance a frequency already felt that is in alignment with it. Aligned frequencies are any of the qualities within the Light described in this book. You can find these in any of the chapter headings.

Gratitude is also a gateway towards reaching these frequencies if we are finding our awareness of our Light has diminished, which can happen when we experience difficult times in life or when life simply starts to feel mundane in the everyday.

It may be difficult to start, because often when our awareness of our Light dims, we can start to feel flat or sad, like something is missing and also feel lonely so it takes a conscious willingness and some level of determination to choose to focus on the things we are grateful for.

If we can manage this, however, gratitude can help give us an experience of upliftment, which in effect is helping us to lift our frequency towards that of the light.

Start with one thing that you are thankful for in your life, one thing that you are able to feel, see or connect to, either within you or around you.

Donna Collins

Notice again the Beauty of nature, your friends, family, children, even the isolated tree by the side of the road, the Beauty of architecture, stained glass, rivers, the rain, blades of grass, clouds, the sun, the moon, physical light that we can see, stars, rainbows, as well as music, laughter, the texture of moss or cotton wool, the smell of wild flowers or cut grass.

Notice and give thanks also to your own sacred meditation space.

Or perhaps your own breath! Or your own consciousness, the gift of awareness of these very things. Don't make it too complicated; simply focus on what is, right now in your life that adds that little bit of Grace – remember this is the oil that makes the engine purr.

It is often very helpful to maintain your gratitude by writing a *GRATITUDE LIST*. This can be done daily.

As I write these words, the song 'Lean on Me' by Bill Withers fills my mind and my heart. As in the song, Gratitude can be seen as a friend, that helping hand that reaches down to lift us up in difficult times or gently supports us, holding us safely in a place we experience as special.

Your focus on experiencing gratitude can be imagined as reaching out for that helping hand, especially when days become difficult. Gratitude is the bringer of hope in the darkness. It is the giver of wings so you can soar in the joy and happiness when days are deemed as 'good'.

The challenge is always to *remember to look outward and reach*. The temptation will always be to make yourself small and shrink into difficult feelings, believing the smallness of yourself. Instead, as we have shared in this book, honouring feelings enough for them to pass, then reaching for your very own helping hand is the way back to experiencing the frequency of your Light.

This practice is one that has been actively encouraged and taught in many organised support groups, particularly for those experiencing hard times in life. Groups such as the AA (Alcoholics Anonymous) advocate this very thing to help people approach every day in a way that is manageable, sustainable and can become enjoyable.

One profound example of how we can miss something very obvious to be grateful for will perhaps have shown itself as you have read this chapter. When the examples were given previously of what you may be grateful for, did you consider also being grateful for simply being YOU?

Whilst you have been busy contending with all your learnt false beliefs about yourself, I wonder if you have ever marvelled at the full extent of the miracle of who you are.

Donna Collins

You are a unique, beautiful, conscious being of Light. This is something to be grateful for! (Or perhaps even reading this book?!)

And so, gratitude can be the ignition to restart your engine, the ignitor of your fire and your flame within as well as the sustainer and intensifier of great feelings. Gratitude is the card you always keep in any card game, and close to your chest. It's yours to use.

When we consider again that feelings are energy moving through the body, we can start to really get to know each feeling for the frequency that it is. This takes practice, but over time, you will fine-tune your ability to feel the subtle difference in the frequency of the energy of the feeling.

We can start to learn that what we focus on grows. A well-known anecdote in spiritual and energetically aware circles is, 'Where attention goes, energy flows.' Gratitude is the card we play to get there and sustain the feeling.

How many times when you feel happy are you ever thankful for feeling this frequency? Gratitude for the frequency of happiness sustains the feeling of happiness, which the energy of the multiverse responds to. Happiness then flows to you with every breath, bringing you more of it!

Being grateful is therefore a means of sustaining and perpetuating an energetic frequency to enable you to feel it more often. *I would recommend practising gratitude for feelings as often as possible.* This really does work!

Gratitude is also something that occurs when there is a realisation within the psyche that it doesn't have to keep striving for more, that it actually has everything it already needs. Gratitude can provide insight, a shift in perspective that alters how your psyche perceives yourself and the world.

It is the nugget that you have been looking for that says, I am already enough, I don't need anything else to prove myself. Gratitude brings the realisation and acknowledgement of everything you already are and already have, right now, in this very moment.

When this happens, gratitude can also be the bearer of not only relief but also peace, a sense of fulfilment and joy.

How is it to imagine that there is simply nothing more to be done? You've already made it.

Rainbow Practices

1. Practise the Mountain Top Gratitude visualisation. Write and draw your experiences

2. Write a daily Gratitude list

3. Remember to look outward and reach for your own helping hand and if you need further help, that of another

4. Practise being grateful for how you feel regularly and if possible DAILY

Chapter Eleven

Being Light in the Everyday

'Eyes when I couldn't see' are words that flowed through me as I started to write this chapter and I was surprised to find that they are part of a song I'd heard years ago and never truly felt in my heart, yet here they were flowing through me in that moment.

I wondered how the words of the song were part of being Light in the everyday. I started to contemplate on the many songs that have been written that are based on loving and being loved by another person. They bring the suggestion that the experience of Faith and being all that we are happens because we are loved by another person.

I then realised that this chapter was about helping others start to believe something different, to start to imagine that life can be different, that Faith and Love could instead come from the experience of allowing the Light within us to be our compass and guide us in everyday life. How wonderful would it be to start to hear songs that are written about our own inner Love?

How is it to acknowledge that you are greater than you imagine you are if *you* love you? And that once you start loving and trusting yourself, this awareness can never leave you.

Ultimately, this creates a beautiful experience of Faith in everyday life and more than that, at a profound spiritual level, an inner knowing and wisdom that you are Love itself.

This book has described many aspects and qualities of the Light within, and some practices to help you to access it, but how do we really utilise this awareness, this felt sense in each day?

First, by recognising that the ego mind is one small part of the experience of being in the body, we can learn to understand that the psyche is only one part of who we are. We can understand that although the psyche helps ensure we survive in this physical existence, it also limits us with false beliefs about ourselves, as described earlier.

Our means of starting to experience more of ourselves is through learning to be with the emotions (the energy in motion) that flow through the body. This is our gateway to experiencing something greater than our thoughts.

We can start to recognise that we are also the temple that is our body, and our emotions are energetic frequencies flowing through us. We can learn to be with our felt sense of these frequencies, with practices, such as the grounding exercise in Chapter 2.

This spectrum of energetic frequencies is termed the Rainbow of Light in this book. The rainbow is also the gateway to the Source of these colourful frequencies, our Light. In simple terms, we access our Light through our emotions.

Once we recognise this, it is possible to really experience a sense of liberation as we practise remembering that when we have what we may have previously experienced as a bad day, in which we may have experienced emotions we may have rejected, we can alter our perception and start to recognise that this is a gift, a doorway to our Light within. I would encourage you to implement a daily practice of reminding yourself that emotions are a gateway to the Light.

We can keep imagining the analogy of ourselves as rays of the sun and the sun being the Source of our light. We are not separate from it; we are part of it and we can learn to listen and align ourselves with the sun or Light in different ways.

Donna Collins

Through meditation, we can practise experiencing the Light within. We can also learn that every time we identify with something that we do, such as being a psychotherapist, we are limiting ourselves. This is because what we *do* is not all that we *are*.

We can also listen to the subtle calling within, our intuition, that takes us closer to our Light. This is experienced by many as things in the physical that we are either gradually drawn to or have a more instant realisation about. This is the call to the expansiveness and creativity of the Source of Light.

For example, there are millions of people who, over more recent years, have been drawn to changing to a healthier diet – literally millions of people who one day decided that somewhere within them they feel they are deserving of something better than, that they are more than, they believed they were. In this instance, the realisation comes through food. This is the start of listening to a voice within that is calling them to be more aligned with their Light.

The feeling that you want to be healthy is a call to stop limiting yourself, to become more expansive, limitless. I would term this a *spark of creativity* – a thought or idea that leads to the creation of change or transformation, both within and externally.

This is the ray of the sun listening and becoming aligned with the sun itself (or the Source). Some would call this the universe when described energetically, or pure consciousness, or some would use the word 'God'.

For most people, the calling is as subtle as deciding to eat better, leaving a relationship that feels stifling and restrictive, being less tied to the happenings of social media, or being kinder and more at one with the planet. Anything that has a sense of needing freedom, more expansion and less restriction can often be a call to Source.

This calling can also be very instant and intense. Many people have experienced spiritual emergence as flow of the unconscious into consciousness in which they have a glimpse into the energetic reality in which we exist. After experiencing this limitless, formlessness, they are called to change their lives completely.

For most, listening to the subtle call – through intuition and allowing yourself to be drawn to the things that feel less restrictive and *lighter* – is the commencement of following a spiritual path to the Light within.

Again, listening is not through the physical ears; it is learning to listen with the heart. We can start by going beyond our physical senses, such as learning to listen to the stillness beyond the sound. This naturally brings a sense of peace and stillness which is the Light. This practice helps us to recognise the difference between heart-based knowing beyond words and listening with the physical senses.

We can also then take our attention to the heart space and within the stillness we have experienced, allow the heart to communicate with us.

Visualisation: Listening to the Stillness

Start again in your sacred meditation space, sitting comfortably and as much as possible ensuring that your back is supported.

Close your eyes and take your attention within. Focus on your breath, breathing right down into your stomach.

Breathe out any tension in your body and as you relax, bring your attention to the sounds around you. You may notice noises in the room that you're in, the street outside and perhaps more distant noises as well as the sound of the birds.

As you sit, noticing these sounds, start to also notice the stillness beyond the sounds; don't try too hard, simply allow the stillness *to come into your awareness. Now notice where in your body you sense this stillness. Breathe in and out of this place.*

Focus your attention on bringing the stillness into your heart space, again not forcing or trying too hard, simply allowing this to happen. When you are experiencing this, practise asking the stillness for guidance. What can help you in your life right now?

Take a few moments to listen with your heart, beyond the words; notice what comes to you, and simply allow.

When you are ready, take a couple of deeper breaths and bring your awareness back to your body, back to the room that you're in and open your eyes.

Once we have the Wisdom through experience of the presence of something greater than ourselves, we can develop our practice of allowing this to flow through our hearts in order to guide us. We can start to experience that the heart space is the two-way portal in which we listen and receive; the flow of energy comes from Source as an intuitive knowing and is manifested through the physical body to create change.

We can learn to trust that when we do this in the everyday, we are being guided along our path. We have our sail gently set so that we are in the energetic flow of our own frequency that will take us where we need to be.

Donna Collins

We can also learn to live a life that is, in some respects, in service – a life in which the ego mind is secondary to soul consciousness. This is what it means to allow rather than to force.

In 'service' means that we understand our soul purpose, and that will always be for the collective good as well as ourselves.

In my practice as a therapist, I trust in this knowing and clients are always brought through an energetic resonance to me and this has remained unchanged whether I have had means, such as a website, to find me or not.

The most important thing is to learn first to live a life that is in alignment with your soul purpose. We get to this level of awareness when we learn to let go of the fear that keeps this hidden from us. When you become aware of your purpose, it is possible to set your intention, your thoughts to that of helping others. This is your primary intention, which in turn helps you.

In my experience, when both soul alignment and intention occur, a further change happens. We move from trusting to *being* Faith. Trusting is necessary on the path, but also suggests a small separation from who we are. I say this because which aspect of you is doing the trusting and which aspect of you is trying to believe?

Being Faith is simply that, *being* it. It's being the Light that you are. Light is not trying to believe in itself. It just is. A flower is not trying to trust, it's a flower. It just *is*! When you start being the spiritual being that you are, external factors change. Work, people, experiences flow to you. Remember the universe flows to you with every breath. Your thoughts are another energetic stream that are either aligned or are not.

If your thoughts are really saying *I don't really believe this but I'll give it a go!* it's not going to happen.

I have heard many people tell me that the law of attraction doesn't work. That's because they may say things out loud and consciously think something but their unconscious beliefs about themselves are not aligned and they don't fully believe. They are not Faith in the everyday.

So once your fears and unconscious beliefs change, life changes. People arrive in your life when you have asked, clients are drawn to you. Transformation happens.

In my practice, I ground my energetic awareness by sitting occasionally with my diary and I will look at when I have availability. I will then set my intention, and I will request, of my own and the collective Light: 'Send me those I can help.'

It's important here never to focus on money, no matter how in need you are. Focus on how you are helping others. This works. Energetically, the universe, or pure consciousness, whatever you want to call it, responds at the frequency that you are literally breathing out at that moment.

The 'turnaround' time for me used to be a couple of months. Now it can happen in a couple of hours or even minutes!

Remember, intention setting can never be for money or material gain, that just happens naturally. This works if your intention is on helping others, which in turn helps yourself.

Remember also, the multiverse knows everything that is in that intention, including your feelings. You cannot lie!

So first, you need to be in alignment with your soul purpose – your work needs to align with this – then your intention must focus on the greater good, helping others. To get this right, practise listening to your heart for your soul purpose as in Chapter 6.

Remember, you are on this planet for a reason… your purpose is to know it and fulfil it.

You can get to this level of awareness and understanding by simply living an 'energetic life'. What I mean by this is to live a life that respects and continuously listens to your energetic state and has awareness that your frequency or vibration will always be responded to by the energy surrounding you, not just in your immediate surroundings but by the entire multiverse.

When we live with this awareness, it is also possible to live with the understanding that our thoughts, which are energy, can also change the biological structure of our bodies, and that of others, whether we are in the same physical space as them or not. We can learn to send distant healing to others as well as heal ourselves.

In a study by Masaru Emoto, a Japanese scientist, thoughts, intentions and feelings were directed into frozen water. When the ice crystals were viewed under a microscope, there was an observed difference in the appearance between the ice crystals sent the intention of love and those sent the feeling of anger.

Human beings are up to 60% water, with the heart and brain being more like 73% water. Imagine how you are affecting your own physical wellbeing at a cellular level just with your thoughts and the emotional or energetic state these create.

It is possible to give yourself healing, simply by intention; send loving thoughts to yourself, imagine your entire body filling with healing Light, the frequency of Love. You can also send your thoughts in the same way to others, sending them Love, knowing that this in turn will come back to you with every breath.

Our developing sense of being connected and at one with a Source greater than ourselves can also allow us to implement other profound life-changing practices to further healing in a way that has transformational effects.

This happens through increasing our awareness of Source, the Divine Light of Creation, as well as our own Light or 'energetic body' and by recognising the importance of our hearts.

Our heart space is a portal or doorway to experiencing a life of expansive, infinite, creative possibilities. Imagine it like a revolving doorway, an energetic portal to receive and experience unconditional Love. It is also the space in which energy is felt in the body as emotions.

When we start to realise that this energy comes from Source itself, it is not a separate feeling that just happens to arrive randomly; we can learn to shift our awareness from the emotion felt in the body to the energy from whence it came.

This is a challenging concept for some; however, one way to understand this is to consider that some spiritual traditions believe that we are all aspects of the Divine or Source, experiencing itself through the physical body.

So how would it be to imagine that the moment in which you accept that you have forgotten all that you are, you can open to the realisation that your experience of the many emotional frequencies in your body are the Light of God experiencing Itself?

Once you become conscious of this huge concept, it is possible to choose to allow the energy of the emotion to release back to Source. This means that it is also possible to instantly release emotions by becoming aware of the energy that is creating it.

This is an immensely profound concept and can be life changing for all those who are able to practise and sense into their own 'energy field' or 'Light'.

For those who are not yet open to this concept, all the other practices in this book will help you to start to experience your own Light within. This will help you become more open and aware of your energy field, which is basically a felt sense of the energy of your own Light outside of you as well as within.

I would also recommend trying some basic energy awareness practices.

Donna Collins

Sensing the Energy Field practice 1

Start by standing, breathing gently; relax your body and ensure you have a gentle bend in your knees.

Now imagine that you are holding a beach ball in front of you, away from your body. Your hands should be about 30cms apart. Close your eyes, then very slowly, bring your hands inwards until you start to become aware of a subtle force, similar to the magnetic field between two magnets.

Stay in this space for a few moments; take your time to feel, it is very subtle so practise a few times.

When you are ready, bring your attention back to the room that you're in; taking a couple of deeper breaths, come back to your body and open your eyes.

This is your energy field! If you are not aware of it to begin with, keep practising this along with the other visualisations in this book.

Sensing the Energy Field practice 2

Again, start by standing. Breathing gently, relax your body and ensure you have a gentle bend in your knees. Now take one of your hands and hold it about 12 inches away from your heart, palm facing towards your heart. Close your eyes, then very slowly, move your hand inwards towards your heart; sense the point at which you feel a slight resistance on your hand, again like the magnetic force between two magnets.

Again, stay in this space for a few moments; take your time to feel, it is very subtle so practise a few times.

When you are ready, bring your attention back to the room that you're in; taking a couple of deeper breaths, come back to your body and open your eyes.

Your awareness of your field will gradually become heightened as you continue with these practices. You may start to become aware that your energy field is not just in front of you from your heart; it is all around you and many people sense this around 12 inches away from their physical body.

Donna Collins

Once you feel more confident with this and for those already open to this concept, I encourage you to implement the following practice into your daily life:

Energetic body self-healing practice

Start by sitting comfortably in a chair or on a cushion, feet flat on the floor or cross-legged. Close your eyes and breathe gently, yet fully, down into your stomach. Notice how your toes feel today whilst continuing to breathe.

Contemplate any particular emotion you have been feeling about a recent situation. Try to relax and allow yourself to feel the emotion in your heart. Now take your awareness to your subtle body, your energy field, and focus on sensing where in your energetic field this emotion is. You may see this as a colour. This is not the feeling itself but the energy creating it.

When you begin to sense this, focus on continuing to breathe fully, allowing yourself to feel the energy. Now, imagine that you are a vessel for the Divine to experience itself, say inwardly 'This is how it feels to experience (whatever the emotion is). Now that I have experienced this, I return it to you with Love.

Notice the changes in your body, focus on your breath and allow your body to release the energy in whatever way happens for you. Take your time.

Give thanks and Love for the experience. Then gently bring your awareness back to your body, back to the room that you're in; focus on the exhale of your breath for a moment, then open your eyes when you are ready. Take time to sit before you stand, ensuring you are grounded back in your body.

It's important not to rush this practice. When you return the energy, you may experience some form of physical reaction in your body. This can be experienced as a release of tension, a feeling of lightness or expansion in your heart, or a feeling similar to waking up suddenly and feeling like you have landed back in your body, like a gentle jolt.

I have also experienced overwhelming laughter and joy as well as continuous burping as I release the energy, which is completely normal!

This can be a hugely transformative healing practice, so after you experience the shift in your body, if you have seen anything visual, any images, ensure you are not drawn to the curiosity of what this is – simply experience and let go. Focus on ensuring that you let the energy go and very gently breathe.

Donna Collins

As you become more practiced at this, it is possible to transmute an emotion when we realise that what is behind it is the loving presence of the Divine. We can start to experience that the energy behind any emotion is the Divine Light of Creation, which is ultimately Love; just as the Light creates a rainbow in the sky, it also creates the rainbow of frequencies felt within you.

Transforming Emotions daily practice

Throughout your day, when you experience emotions, it's always important to honour your feeling. Each time an emotion is felt, start by telling yourself it's OK to feel this. I honour the feeling of (whatever the emotion is).

Close your eyes if it is safe to do so and if you feel you need to. Be aware of the feeling of the emotion in your body, then focus your attention beyond your own energy field to the expansiveness of the Divine energy behind the feeling, which is always a place of Love. This is the Light creating the feeling, which is the Rainbow of experience in your body.

Breathe with the emotion; breathe in and breathe out. Feel the emotion first and then continue breathing until you are able to sense the Love behind it.

Allow yourself to spend a moment really being with and becoming that Love. When you have really felt this through your body and the original emotion has passed, open your eyes and continue with your day!

This is a daily practice which will continue to heighten your awareness of the Loving energy that you are. This in turn will help you increase your awareness of your heart as the place where this energy transforms into emotions.

Many people have learnt the concept of the heart as a portal and have both learnt to sense energy for energetic healing practices as well as to transmute the energy received by the heart into conscious communication, both verbal and written.

Many inspiring speakers and successful entrepreneurs have created their world through this realisation, and their words carry a sense of Truth that is able to emotionally 'touch' those who listen and feel its presence. Being Light in the everyday is learning to let this energy flow through you. I encourage you to practise allowing yourself to open and surrender your heart to enable you to speak your Truth.

As you now know, Truth is another word for Light. Let your Light speak and express itself through your heart every day, in every interaction.

Rainbow Practices

1. Implement a daily practice to remind yourself that emotions are a gateway to the Light

2. Practise noticing your own subtle inner call to the Light by noticing what you are drawn to in each day

3. Practise the Listening to the Stillness visualisation

4. Practise Sensing the Energy Field 1 & 2

5. Practise energetic body self-healing

6. Use the Transforming Emotions daily practice

Chapter Twelve

Being Faith

Ultimately, Faith as I described at the start of this book, is living fearlessly, 'Going boldly with Trust in your Heart.' Now with more knowledge, it is possible to understand and start to experience that Trust is actually Truth (Light) in your heart.

This book has shown you the steps to get there. Faith becomes about simply being that which you are without any sense of separation. It's fully and fearlessly, expansively and joyously, lovingly and acceptingly LIVING.

To start, in my experience, and as many spiritual traditions believe, one thing needs to happen. This is another universal law, the Law of Inspired Action, which suggests that we also need to take action in order for something bigger to respond.

This is what the Sufis call 'the pathless path'. This means that everything is there for you in the multiverse right now. In order for this to happen, you need to take the first step. Only then will the path appear.

Donna Collins

So right now, you can choose. You have the tools through this book to do just that.

This book is a reflection of my own spiritual journey, years of psychotherapy and an intense spiritual awakening as I searched for 'all that I am' to realise that 'I am all that is.'

When I really sat with this realisation, I found myself wondering and writing the following from my heart: *Do we really have to go through all of that? All of that seeking to come right back to all that we knew as children? To live... Is that a life lost almost or something gained?*

I realised that the point is that this time we can do it consciously. With new-found awareness of the exact reason we are here. We can live, without distraction, and flow in the energy of life, as the children we once were but this time do it all consciously. We can make the choice in every moment that we take a breath.

So I advocate to laugh and feel joy in the simplicity of being the most complex creation you could ever imagine but endeavour to catch yourself in time, before you imagine too much, before your mind starts analysing, and simply live with all the complexity in its most simple form.

I encourage anyone who is reading this book to always hold in mind that the journey you are on is completely necessary, and implementing the practices in this book is the first step on the pathless path.

I also gently advise to always remember that spiritual seeking is like glimpsing a mouse under your floorboards and never being able to catch it. You know it's there, it's exciting, and also a little scary that it lives with you, but eventually you realise that if you spend all your time looking for it, you will stop living your life. So practise and then live! Simply Be It!

Remember that your purpose is to experience life at its fullest, through every aspect of your being, in the full greatness of all that you are. This way of viewing life means that there is no place for regret as you can live with the Wisdom that you are here to experience every facet of every emotion, the *Rainbow of Light as the doorway to the Source of who you are.*

Donna Collins

The following words flowed through my heart as I began to write the ending of this book:

> I Am The One
> The Eternal Being
> The Presence Of Breath & Life
> The Stillness & Profound Beauty
> Residing In You As Eternal Love
> And The Light Of Everlasting Consciousness
> I Am The Love
> That I Am

If you can be aware of this in the everyday, then the journey of exploration and seeking is complete. I wish everyone who implements the practices and concepts in this book, the heartfelt openness and wonderment of this experience.

Bibliography

Alexander, C. F. (1848). 'All Things Bright and Beautiful.' Hymn.
Boberg, C. (1885). 'How Great Thou Art.' Hymn.
Coelho, P. (1992). *The Alchemist*, translated by Alan R. Clarke. London: HarperCollins Publishers.
Davies, W. H. (1911). 'Leisure.' *Songs Of Joy and Others*, Oxford: A. C. Fifield.
Durgananda, S. (2002). *The Heart of Meditation: Pathways to a Deeper Experience*. New York: SYDA Foundation.
Emoto, M. (2004). *The Hidden Messages in Water*, translated by David A. Thayne. New York: Atria Books.
John of the Cross, St., E. Allison Peers, and Silverio, of St. Teresa. (2003). *Dark Night of the Soul*. Mineola, NY: Dover Publications.
Jung, C. G. (1922). 'The Tree of Life.' *Red Book - Liber Novus*. Red Book Prints.
Newton, J. (1779). 'Amazing Grace.' Hymn.
Oxford English Dictionary, Oxford: Oxford University Press.
Winnicott, D. W. (1960). 'Ego distortion in terms of true and false self.' *The Maturational Process and the Facilitating Environment: Studies in the Theory of Emotional Development*. New York: International Universities Press, Inc, pp. 140–57.
Withers, B. (1972) 'Lean On Me,' *Still Bill*. Sussex Records.

Printed in Great Britain
by Amazon